IMAGES OF
PLYMOUTH &
SOUTH DEVON
RAILWAYS

IMAGES OF
PLYMOUTH & SOUTH DEVON RAILWAYS

CLASSIC PHOTOGRAPHS FROM
THE MAURICE DART RAILWAY COLLECTION

HALSGROVE

First published in Great Britain in 2007

British Library Cataloguing-in-Publication Data
A CIP record for this title is available from the British Library

ISBN 978 1 84114 514 3

HALSGROVE
Halsgrove House
Ryelands Farm Industrial Estate, Bagley Green,
Wellington, Somerset TA21 9PZ
Tel: 01823 653777   Fax: 01823 216796
email: sales@halsgrove.com
website: www.halsgrove.com

Printed and bound by
CPI Antony Rowe Ltd., Chippenham, Wiltshire

CONTENTS

INTRODUCTION

An interest in railways was bred in me from my very early days when, in the pram, as well as cuddly woolly dogs, I had a small wooden engine to hold. As I grew, a larger metal engine replaced the earlier toy. My grandmother lived with us at Stoke, Devonport, and she would take me out each morning to a nearby park where I was shown trains crossing a viaduct. Sometimes she would take me on to the platform at Dockyard Halt. Following a move to St Budeaux, by which time I rode in a pushchair, the morning trips were usually down the hill to sit on the GWR station for an hour or so. Before I commenced attending school and could read or write, we would see up to three named engines pass through and I was taught to memorise their names. When my father came home to dinner, I would tell him their names, which he wrote in a notebook. Apparently, my grandfather had served in the Royal Engineers as an engine driver during the South African and Boer Wars and afterwards in Britain, which explains my grandmother's interest. We also had an O gauge Hornby railway in the house, which gradually expanded as I grew up.

Most Saturday afternoons my parents would take me with them to either Devonport, reached by tram, or Plymouth, for which we caught a motor train to Millbay. So my interest in railways steadily developed. During the summers of 1937, 1938 and 1939, the three of us spent a week travelling by train to Torquay, Paignton or Goodrington, with sometimes a venture to Kingswear and across to Dartmouth on the *Mew*, or to Dawlish Warren. We used a family holiday runabout ticket for the week and set out from St Budeaux on an excursion train that ran daily from Saltash to Paignton and which, from memory, was usually hauled by a Castle class loco-motive to Newton Abbot. My father would also bring home books about railways. They had been loaned to him for me to look at; they contained many photographs of railway subjects. During the Second World War, I was evacuated to Bude, by train from Friary. This was followed by a period at St Austell, using trains to and from North Road. Whilst there, at the evacuated Grammar school, I met many older boys who were railway enthusiasts and my 'railway educa-tion'commenced properly.

My father had been transferred to the Dockyard at Gibraltar during 1944, and in the summer of 1947 I went there by sea for a holiday for several weeks. My father was an amateur photographer and whilst I was there he taught me to use a box camera. I immediately started taking photographs of Gibraltar Dockyard locomotives from a balcony!

On returning to St Budeaux I found my father's two old cameras and managed to obtain a film for each. A large folding Kodak that used A-122 film turned out to have a pin hole in the bellows, only discovered when the results of the first film were seen, This made it unuseable. The other was an old Box Brownie, which had a push over lever shutter release, and had one good and one faulty viewfinder that showed two images, one above the other. I persevered with this, but did not know enough to achieve much success. I tried to record trains passing through St Budeaux and went to Laira shed, late in September, and took photos, some against the low evening sun. Still, we all had to learn by experience. This was the start of my collection of railway photographs.

As time progressed I was able to buy better cameras and commenced longer railway trips to places further afield. My railway interest widened from purely collecting engine names and numbers, to encompass signalling and railway history. This was progressed by meeting more and more very knowledgeable older railway enthusiasts and railwaymen, many of whom became great friends of mine. I developed a desire to obtain photographs of some of the locomotives that I had seen in my early years, so the process of searching for and purchasing photos commenced. As my interest and knowledge grew, so likewise did the quest for more photos. This now encompassed all of Devon and Cornwall, and large sections of Wales, along with various classes of locomotives from all over the country. An interest in narrow gauge and industrial railways developed. So the 'Archive' steadily grew from filling an expanding suitcase to occupying a considerable expanse of shelf space.

When it was suggested that I compile some books making use of some of these images I thought that it would be a great idea, as many of them, to the best of my knowledge, had not previously been used in publications.

This book covers Plymouth and South Devon, the boundary being the area south of a line drawn west from the mouth of the River Exe. The northern limits being Dawlish Warren, Heathfield and Mary Tavy. This includes the large railway centres of Newton Abbot and Plymouth, along with the much recorded sea wall at Dawlish and Hemerdon and Dainton banks. With so many photos available the choice has been difficult, but constraints such as copyright and previous use have been considered. I have not included many frquently photographed locations. Many older historic images are included, but I have attempted to give a good overall coverage of the area from around 1900 to the present day. I have included a few diesels and industrial scenes, to attempt to cater for all interests. So many photographs of the preservation era have been published that I have avoided this period with one exception. I have also included some items which are not photographically perfect, but are worthy of insertion because of their content. There are also a couple of the results that I obtained from my very early days of photography, which nowadays reflect some nostalgia. Some of the period scenes include infrastructure and locomotives 'brand new' ex Works. These images may be of great interest to modellers of historic locomotives with period layouts. The variety of different locomotive types recorded has rendered it impossible to include sections portraying stations, sidings, signal boxes, tunnels and viaducts.

As this, and, hopefully subsequent books, will feature images from my personal collection, the layout follows the order in which the collection is arranged. This follows locomotive wheel arrangement and types from the largest downwards, in decreasing order of size, with a few exceptions. This is a system that was used in the past by several notable authors. It presents a markedly different layout to the now standard practice of following routes geographically. Readers seeking photos at specific locations should refer to the index of locations at the end of the book.

I have attempted to make the captions detailed without delving too deeply into railway history or becoming too technical. Any errors that are discovered are purely attributable to myself. I trust that within the contents there is material to cater for most railway interests, and that happy memories of a bygone age of railways will be recalled.

ACKNOWLEDGEMENTS

I express special thanks to my friend of many years, Mike Daly, and also to Kenneth Brown, for permission to reproduce photos taken by them. Likewise I express thanks for permission to use photos which I have purchased from the collections of the Stephenson Locomotive Society, The Locomotive Club of Great Britain (Ken Nunn collection) and Rail Archive Stephenson (Photomatic). Also my thanks and apologies are proffered to other photographers whose work has been used and not credited. Where no credit is given the photographer is unknown. I also extend my thanks to Steve Jenkins for advice when describing some of the earlier coaching stock and to Jill Green for checking the proofs and for suggesting amendments.

REFERENCE SOURCES

A Detailed History of British Railways Standard Steam Locomotives. RCTS.
A Regional history of the Railways of Great Britain. Vol.1. The West Country.
David St.John Thomas. David & Charles.
Branch Line To Kingsbridge. Vic Mitchell and Keith Smith. Middleton Press.
Branch Line To Kingswear. Vic Mitchell and Keith Smith. Middleton Press.
British Railways Locomotive Stock Changes and Withdrawal Dates. 1948 –1968.
Michael McManus.
British Railways Steam Locomotives 1948 – 1968. Hugh Longworth. OPC.
GWR Locomotive Allocations. J.W.P. Rowledge. David & Charles.
Locomotives of the Great Western Railway. RCTS.
Locomotives of the LBSCR. D.L.Bradley. RCTS.
Locomotives of the LSWR. D.L.Bradley. RCTS.
Locomotives of the Southern Railway. D.L.Bradley. RCTS.
Newton Abbot To Plymouth. Vic Mitchell & Keith Smith. Middleton Press.
The Allocation History of BR Diesels & Electrics. Roger Harris.
Track Layout Diagrams of the GWR/BRWR. South Devon. R.A.Cooke.
My personal notebooks dating from 1945.

STANDARD 2-10-0s

These large locos were comparative newcomers to the scene as construction was not started until January 1954 and none appeared in Devon until the years 1959-60, at which point dieselisation was commencing. Hence their stay in the area was of short duration, with Laira receiving a small allocation for a short period. They proved to be versatile and were utilised to work additional passenger trains at times on summer Saturdays.

The afternoon Penzance to Kensington milk train departs from Plymouth North Road and passes Mutley during 1960, hauled by 92238 which was shedded at Old Oak Common, London. With a lightly loaded train this powerful loco did not require an assistant loco. The loco is looking rather uncared for.   Mike Daly

A down fitted goods comes through Brent headed by 92218 from St Phillips Marsh shed, Bristol, in the early 1960s. The branch line to Kingsbridge heads off to the right. Trains composed like this are but a memory and it is pleasing to see semaphore signals and ground discs in use.

2
EIGHT COUPLED ENGINES

This section includes the well respected GWR 2800 and 2884 class 2-8-0s, which were capable of hauling trains of one hundred loaded coal wagons, along with the R.O.D.s and 4700s. Also included are the GWR eight coupled tanks, along with LMS 8F and WD 2-8-0s.

For a while during 1951-52 St Blazey shed had one or more 7200 class 2-8-2Ts allocated. The longest resident of these was 7209, which is heading a Tavistock Junction to St Blazey goods past St Budeaux West refuge loop. The roof of the long vanished signal box is visible above the third van. Mike Daly

Newton Abbot shed had between three and five members of the 7200 class on their books in the early 1950s, and here 7220 departs from Aller loop on a down goods in 1950, with banking assistance being provided by a 5101 class 2-6-2T. The author first saw this loco when it appeared at St Austell on a Sunday afternoon in 1944, bearing an LLY (Llanelly) shed stencil.

One of the earlier batch of 2800 class 2-8-0s, 2834 is in the yard behind the coaler at Laira shed. Trackwork is underway in the background, so this could be in 1931 when the shed was undergoing expansion.

Despite being classed as Heavy Goods locos, the 28s/38s were sometimes utilised to handle summer Saturday extra trains. This unusual photo shows 3815, which is one of the later 2884 class locos, heading a stopping passenger train at Dawlish Warren in 1949. The loco was shedded at Severn Tunnel Junction and may have been borrowed by Bath Road shed, Bristol. Kenneth Brown

A train of empty coaching stock (ECS) heading for either Paignton or Kingswear is taken out of Newton Abbot by 2884 class 2-8-0 3834, from Exeter shed, on 28 August 1955. As this was a Wednesday, the stock must have been for a summer extra working.

The nine large 2-8-0s of the 4700 class were designed to work fast vacuum fitted perishable traffic and were rarely seen at work during the main part of the day. Awaiting coaling at Laira shed in September 1928 is 4701 with a Duke class 4-4-0 behind it. This loco has the snifting valves fitted on the outside of the steam chests and has a small capacity tender.

Here we see the last member of the class, 4708, at Newton Abbot on passenger stock on 20 June 1961. The train is probably a summer weekday extra working. This Old Oak Common based loco has a large capacity tender and snifting valves on the frame behind the steampipes.   J.H.Meredith

During the First World War 521 locos were built for the Railway Operating Division of the Royal Engineers for service in France. The design was similar to Robinson locos on the Great Central Railway. When hostilities ended the GWR purchased some and others were received on loan. They were popularly known as R.O.D.s. Some were returned and others were rebuilt and modified by the GWR, but many were withdrawn before the Second World War. Standing on the outlet from Newton Abbot shed, on an unknown date after 1944, is 3025 from Stafford Road shed, Wolverhampton. The building in the background is the GWR wagon works.   B.M. Barber.

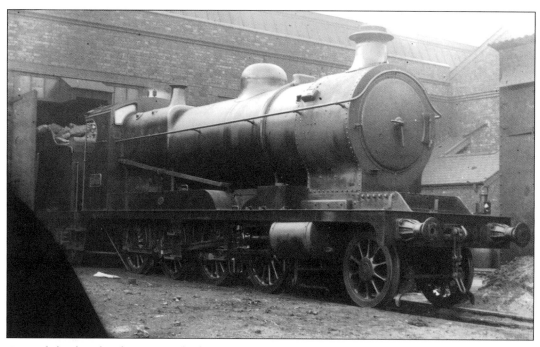

One of the batch of R.O.Ds which was purchased in 1925, fitted with fluted casings to the buffers, is 3040 which is standing outside one of the entrances to the roundhouse at Laira in the late 1920s. A.G. Ellis

During the Second World War a requirement for heavy goods locos to work both at home and overseas was met by the four railway companies building batches of LMS Stanier 8F 2-8-0s. The batch built at Swindon worked first on the GWR, after which they were returned to the LMS. After the formation of British Railways in January 1948 several of the locos returned to operate on the Western Region and one of these, 48459, which was shedded at St Phillips Marsh, Bristol, stands on the outlet from Newton Abbot shed on 16 September 1956. One of the locos, for assisting over the South Devon banks, 5183, is standing in front of the 8F.

In addition to the LMS 8F design, a large number of locos were built to a somewhat similar design for the War Department, and were known as WDs or 'Austerities'. One of these, 90251 from St Phillips Marsh shed, is running alongside the River Plym and is about to pass under the Embankment Road bridge to enter Laira shed, after working a goods train into Tavistock Junction yard in the early 1950s. A splendid group of signals are in this scene.   Mike Daly

The GWR developed a tank loco version of the 2800 class 2-8-0s. They were mostly to be found in South Wales, but from the late 1930s St Blazey shed usually had one or two. One long resident member was 4200 class 2-8-0T 4298, seen in ex Works condition, which is climbing Dainton bank with a goods for Tavistock Junction yard in the early 1950s. A large Prairie tank is providing assistance at the rear.   J.W. Whitnall

3

PACIFIC 4-6-2s

Until the Southern Railway introduced the West Country class Light Pacifics in 1945, locos with this wheel arrangement were virtually unknown west of Exeter, apart from very rare visits on special trains over the GWR route. Their arrival saw the faithful N class locos relegated to work goods trains, but the T9s continued to work some passenger trains over the North Cornwall line. With the arrival of BR Standard 'Britannia' class locos in 1951 this type were regularly seen in the area, and Laira gained some on allocation for a time.

The Southern Railway introduced the 'Merchant Navy' class Pacifics during 1941 to work heavy express passenger trains from Waterloo to Exeter and Bournemouth. They were too heavy to work over the SR routes west of Exeter, but on 20 September 1958 one of the rebuilt locos, 35023 'HOLLAND AFRIKA LINE', from Exmouth Junction shed, worked a special train over the GWR route to Plymouth. It is seen in the yard at Laira shed, having been coaled and watered, ready for the return working. Mike Steer

Another unusual working occurred on 3 May 1964 when Plymouth Railway Circle, in conjunction with the Railway Correspondence & Travel Society, ran a special steam hauled train from Exeter St Davids to Penzance and back. 'West Country' class light Pacific 34002 'SALISBURY', shedded at Eastleigh, is waiting at Plymouth North Road to take 'The Cornubian' to Penzance. This was the last steam working into Cornwall, at the time, by a type never before seen west of Truro on the GWR route.

When built, the 'West Country' class carried numbers in a system developed by their designer, O.V.S. Bulleid. Also, to retain route familiarisation in case of diversions, certain trains over the GWR and SR routes between Plymouth and Exeter were worked by the other companies' locos and crews. During June 1948 21C125 'WHIMPLE' from Exmouth Junction shed, passes along the sea wall between Teignmouth and Dawlish with an up WR train. The leading vehicle appears to be one of the GWR Stores vans, ex Royal train clerestory stock.   L.R. Peters

Another Exmouth Junction loco, rebuilt 'West Country' 34024 'TAMAR VALLEY', engulfes the platform and surrounding area at Plymouth North Road with steam as it awaits departure on 9 March 1963.

A series of locomotive exchanges to compare performances took place during 1925. Here is a very rare record of LNER A10 class 4474 'VICTOR WILD' entering Plymouth North Road at 6.40pm on the 1.30pm from Paddington, which was the first trial run, on 20 April. Note the original overline bridge and East signal box.   Stephenson Locomotive Society

BR 'Britannia' class 70024 'VULCAN' pilots a 'King' class 4-6-0 into Plymouth North Road on an express from Paddington in the early 1950s. The train could well be the second part (relief train) of the 'Limited'(Cornish Riviera). 0-6-0 PT 6419 waits in a siding with a two coach Auto train for Saltash. Mike Daly

4

KING AND CASTLE CLASS 4-6-0s

These were the elite of GWR locomotives and handled most of the faster timed express passenger trains on the system. As they were heavier than a Castle, the Kings were, for many years, only permitted to travel on the routes from Paddington to Wolverhampton, Bristol and Plymouth. They were 'Double Red' in the GWR's route restriction colour system. The Castles were spread widely throughout the system, apart from in Central Wales. Members of both classes were capable of attaining over 100mph under the right conditions.

On 8 September 1928 an immaculate 6005 'KING GEORGE III' stands at the head of an up passenger train at Plymouth North Road. The dimensions of the special front bogie fitted to these locos is apparent.

In the mid-1950s the down 'Limited', the 10.30am Paddington to Penzance, races through Totnes to mount the bank to Tigley and Rattery. It is 'super powered', being hauled by 'Britannia' class Pacific 70015 'APOLLO', from Old Oak Common shed, which is piloted by Laira's 6008 'KING JAMES II'. The King would have rendered assistance from Newton Abbot.

The year of 1935 saw the centenary of the GWR celebrated. At this time the LMS and the LNER were competing with each other for the Scottish traffic, and were experimenting with streamlining locos to help to achieve higher speeds on the long runs from London. The GWR tried semi-streamlining one King and one Castle, not necessarily to improve speed, but to reduce the resistance to airflow and hence reduce fuel consumption. 6014 'KING HENRY VII' from Old Oak Common shed, stands beneath the coaler at Newton Abbot shed during August 1937. Streamline skirting that covered the front and sides of the bogie have been removed. The 'bulletnose' was removed by January 1943.

Standing in the yard at its home shed at Laira is 6029 'KING EDWARD VIII' with a 'Castle' to its rear, possibly 5079 'LYSANDER', also based at Laira, during 1948. The King's tender has had the legend 'BRITISH RAILWAYS' applied. but BR shed codes had not been introduced and the loco carries an LA stencil on the side of the frame to the rear of the front buffer. Kenneth Brown

On 17 June 1946, the 8.25am Paddington to Paignton express, hauled by 4097 'KENILWORTH CASTLE', ran into the rear of a goods train near Lawes bridge, north of Torre. The goods train was stopped, waiting for a parcels train to clear Torre station, and a signalling error occurred. The front carriage telescoped over the loco's tender. Mike Daly collection

Standing under the hoist outside its home shed at Laira in the late 1920s is 5004 'LLANSTEPHAN CASTLE'. The loco has a small capacity tender, as originally fitted. A snowplough is on the other side of the loco. Part of the structure of Laira Halt is visible to the right of the loco's smokebox.

Very recently converted from a Star class to a Castle class was 4009 'SHOOTING STAR' which, in 1925, is standing in the yard at Laira where it was shedded, amongst many loco coal wagons. During 1936 this engine was renamed and renumbered, becoming 100 A1 'LLOYDS'. A.G. Ellis

The other semi-streamlined GWR loco, 5005 'MANORBIER CASTLE', enters Newton Abbot on a down express during July 1936. The leading vehicle in the train is a Syphon G van.

Although not photographically perfect by any means, this view, taken on 4 March 1961, is included because it shows a rarely recorded location. Taken against the light from a moving train it shows 'Castle' 5055 'EARL OF ELDON', from Old Oak Common shed, in the loco servicing sidings that were situated in the triangle of lines west of North Road station, Plymouth. The turntable is in the background as are the bridges over the two routes to Millbay. Maurice Dart

The weighing shed at Newton Abbot works was situated between the main works building and the station. For most of the time nothing was visible near it, but during August 1956 'Castle' 5082 'SWORDFISH' was hoisted off its front bogie. The loco, from Old Oak Common shed, was named 'POWIS CASTLE' until January 1941.

An undated scene at Newton Abbot with 5088 'LLANTHONY ABBEY' from Stafford Road shed, Wolverhampton, on the 3.20pm Paddington to Kingswear express. The loco is fitted with one of the new slab sided tenders. Stopped in platform one, on a stopping train to Plymouth, working a route familiarisation turn, is 'West Country' class 34016 'BODMIN' from Exmouth Junction shed. J. Davenport

Diversions took place over the SR route between Plymouth and Exeter on 11 November 1956, due to an overturned crane near Dainton. This extremely rare photo shows Laira's 5098 'CLIFFORD CASTLE' hauling the 4.10pm Plymouth to Paddington on the SR line through St Budeaux Victoria Road. The loco would have been specially authorised to work over the route. Mike Daly

This is another unusual viewpoint by the loco servicing sidings. This post 1957 scene shows 7003 'ELMLEY CASTLE', from Old Oak Common shed, taking a set of empty coaching stock from North Road down around the curve to Millbay.

On 9 May 1964 a special train, chartered by Ian Allan, worked to Plymouth and was to be the last steam hauled train from Plymouth. Old Oak Common's 7029 'CLUN CASTLE', fitted with a double chimney, was to work it and first went on shed at Laira, where it seen being prepared for the run.

On the same day, the author had to work at Bugle during the morning. After a quick lunch I returned by train to Plymouth and used buses to and from home at Honicknowle, and out to Plympton, from where I walked to the top of Hemerdon bank. After about ten minutes 7029 'CLUN CASTLE' breasted the summit and burst under the bridge with the Ian Allan special, in fine style. Maurice Dart

5

HALL, GRANGE AND MANOR CLASS 4-6-0s

Standing at Plymouth North Road is 4902 'ALDENHAM HALL' with another Hall behind it. The date is unspecified but is probably around 1930, as the loco was shedded at Penzance when newly built in 1928. The section of overall roof that covered parts of platforms two and three can be seen; these were served by a common single line. The locos are standing on the centre road between platforms four and five.

At the head of a down stopping train at Torquay is 4906 'BRADFIELD HALL' shortly after it was built in 1929, as it is fitted with a small capacity tender. The train is mainly composed of short clerestory roofed carriages. The signal box which is prominent is still extant, although disused.

This is rare photo of 4911 'BOWDEN HALL' entering Plymouth North Road with a down stopping train when the loco was barely a month old in March 1929. In this, and the preceding two photos, the front lamp bracket on the loco is atop of the smokebox, whereas in later days it was positioned at the top of the front of the smokebox door. This loco was badly damaged during one of the Blitz raids on Plymouth in 1941. However this loco was seen many times by the author, either passing through St Budeaux or at Millbay. Stephenson Locomotive Society

Here is the same loco at Keyham on 29 April 1941 after the Blitz raid during the previous night. A bomb fell alongside the loco, which was subsequently condemned and cut up. The loco had recently been transferred from Laira to Truro. The author recalls his father returning home from fire-watching duties and stating that "There is an engine blown on to the platform at Keyham and a bus upside down on the roof of Milehouse depot". Luckily the crew escaped injury, as they had taken shelter beneath the steps of the signal box. The tender was repaired and ran attached to various locos. Great Western Railway

Another of the early batch of Halls, 4913 'BAGLAN HALL', from Laira shed, is standing alongside Newton Abbot locomotive works on the line to the coaler. The date is unspecified but is soon after the loco entered service in 1929. W. Vaughan-Jenkins

A photograph taken at Laira shed late in 1962, or early in 1963, has one of its own locos, 4978 'WESTWOOD HALL' coming on to the coaling line. To its right, outside the new diesel depot, is 204 HP shunter D2177, recently transferred to Laira following the closure of the SR shed at Friary. A Warship diesel is behind the hoist, which had been transferred to the diesel depot from the steam shed. Mike Daly

This is a very rare photo, taken on 18 May 1955, when ex LMS 'Princess Coronation' class Pacific 46237 'CITY OF BRISTOL', from Camden shed, worked the up 'Limited' from Plymouth, which included a dynamometer car. The train was assisted over the South Devon banks by 5915 'TRENTHAM HALL' from Penzance shed. The photo, which was taken against the light in a strong cross wind, shows the train breasting Dainton bank before entering the tunnel.

A fine action shot shows the up 'Limited' leaving Plymouth North Road on 22 September 1948, hauled by Old Oak Common's 6009 *King Charles II*, and piloted by Laira's 6913 *Levens Hall*. The section of overall roof and the roofs of the station lifts are prominent. The rebuilt North Road East signal box is on the right.

This is one of the batch of Halls which entered service un-named during the Second World War, with the side windows of the cab replaced by sheet metal to prevent glare from the fire acting as a guide for enemy aircraft. It was allocated to Newton Abbot and is at the station on an up goods on 8 September 1947. The loco was later named 'BEACHAMWELL HALL'.

An undated photo of 6813 'EASTBURY GRANGE' at Dainton summit after providing banking assistance for a train going up the bank. From the appearance of the loco, which was shedded at Newton Abbot, the photo was taken shortly after 1945. The Granges were fitted with driving wheels of 5ft 8in diameter, which made them excellent locos for handling trains on West Country gradients. G.E.M. Oldham

After the Second World War, this loco, 6819 'HIGHNAM GRANGE', was shedded at Birkenhead and was regarded as one of the two rarest members of the class at Plymouth. However, the author did see it once on Laira shed stencilled BHD; it was transferred to Banbury in 1948 and is approaching Laira Junction on 24 April of that year on a down express.
Stephenson Locomotive Society

An unusual scene with 6829 'BURMINGTON GRANGE', from Newton Abbot, shed taking an up express from St Budeaux along the SR route to Plymouth North Road on 11 November 1956. The engine had brought the train up from Penzance and reversed over the wartime connection to gain the SR line. This was due to the GW route being blocked by permanent way work. Mike Daly

On Summer Saturdays the locomotive department was hard pressed to find enough engines to work the full service of normal and extra trains, so 2-8-0s were often used. On 19 July 1958 large 2-8-0 4701 from Old Oak Common worked the down 'Royal Duchy' from Paddington and has left Newton Abbot, where it gained assistance from Oxley's 6839 'HEWELL GRANGE'. D.S.Fish

When the faithful old Bulldog class 4-4-0s were transferred away from Laira and Newton Abbot, they were replaced on piloting duties over the banks by lightweight Manors. In the early 1950s Laira's 7804 'BAYDON MANOR' pilots a King up Hemerdon bank on the 3.45pm from Plymouth North Road to Liverpool, which started from Penzance at 12.00 noon and conveyed a postal carriage from Plymouth and through coaches for Manchester London Road.

A down parcels train headed by Laira's 7820 'DINMORE MANOR', has crossed Weston Mill viaduct and is approaching St Budeaux East in the mid 1950s. The dark coloured vehicle towards the centre of the train is a Syphon H van. The branch line to M.O.D. Bullpoint is in foreground. This was one of the later batch of Manors that entered traffic at the end of 1950. Mike Daly

6

STAR CLASS 4-6-0s

The first member of this class was built in 1906 as a 4-4-2 to enable comparisons to be made with the French De Glehn compound 4-4-2s that the GWR had purchased. All of the other class members were built as 4-6-0s, and the first member was converted to that wheel arrangement during November 1909. The class soon proved to be excellent reliable thoroughbreds and, with the Saint class, were responsible for working the principal passenger trains on the GWR system. Several were later converted to Castle class and most of the other members were modified over the years. There usefulness was proved by forty eight passing into BR ownership in January 1948.

Here is the first loco in the class, No.40, at Plymouth North Road very soon after entering service in April 1906, as it has not been named. This engine had a higher platform than subsequent members, together with many mechanical detail differences. It has the 4-4-2 wheel arrangement and one suspects it is on trial owing to the presence of the bowler hatted gentleman standing by the watering point. From his attire, and the fact that he is holding some papers and talking to the engine's crew, it would suggest that he was probably a Locomotive Inspector. A Dean 4-4-0 is partly visible on the right.

After running for a few months No.40 gained the famous name 'NORTH STAR', and here it has been placed at the outlet of the yard at Laira shed for photographs to be taken. The coal supply in the tender has been replenished.

At Torquay, at the head of down passenger stock in 1922, is Laira's 4002 'EVENING STAR'. Compare this view with the previous photo of 'NORTH STAR'. Locomotive Club of Great Britain Ken Nunn collection

Standing at Plymouth North Road, awaiting the road to back out to Laira on 26 July 1924, is 4006 'RED STAR', from Old Oak Common shed. The fireman appears to be noting that the Ground Disc (Dummy) has come off, permitting them to depart. Stephenson Locomotive Society

A member of the crew poses on 4009 'SHOOTING STAR' which is in the yard at Millbay shed, Plymouth, in 1907, the year that the engine was built; it is in brand new condition. The front of the carriage shed can be seen in the left background.

Another immaculate brand new engine in the shed yard at Millbay in 1908, is 4012 'KNIGHT OF THE THISTLE' which was a visitor from Old Oak Common shed, having worked a train down from Paddington.

Stopped at Dawlish at the head of a down express is 4017 *Knight of Liege*, probably in the 1920s. This engine had been named *Knight of the Black Eagle* prior to August 1914. The leading vehicle in the train is a GWR Concertina brake carriage, painted in crimson lake livery. A.G.Ellis

Waiting outside the up end of Newton Abbot station is 4021 *The British Monarch*. This engine was named *King Edward* until June 1927 and the name was altered again to *British Monarch* in October or November 1927, which pins the date of the photo down to within a few months. The engine was shedded at Bath Road, Bristol. A.G.Ellis

Standing in the yard at Newton Abbot shed, with the driver watching the photographer, is 4023 *The Danish Monarch* from Old Oak Common shed. This engine underwent four changes of name, being called *King George* until July 1927. Then in October or November of that year it became *Danish Monarch* and was de-named in November 1940. So, once again, the date of the photo is narrowed down to within a few months. 4018 *Knight of the Grand Cross* is in the background to the right.

At Plymouth North Road, on 3 September 1921, at the head of the 2nd up 'Limited' (relief train) is 4024 *King James* from Old Oak Common shed. A .'Duke'. class 4 - 4 - 0 has been attached to the front as pilot loco to Newton Abbot. This engine was renamed *The Dutch Monarch* in September 1927, and *Dutch Monarch* in September or October of the same year.
P.J.T.Reed

FOUR 'STARS' AT LAIRA SHED

At the throat of the shed yard in 1912 is 4037 'QUEEN PHILIPPA'. This engine was withdrawn in June 1926 and was rebuilt to a 'Castle' class.

At almost the same spot, in 1912, is 4038 'QUEEN BERENGARIA'. As the tender is empty, the engine is waiting to come 'on shed' for servicing.

Again, at the same spot, but in 1911, the year the engine was built, is 4039 'QUEEN MATILDA'.

Once again, at the same position, the driver is at the controls and is watching the photographer recording 4042 'PRINCE ALBERT', on which two of the shed's engine disposal staff are posed. The immaculate condition of the engine suggests a date in 1913, shortly after it entered service.

A crowd of curious onlookers survey the scene, and also watch the photographer, at Dawlish, after 4049 'PRINCESS MAUD', hauling a passenger train, ran into the rear of a goods train in 1918.

Laira's 4054 'PRINCESS CHARLOTTE' is north of St Budeaux, as it works one of the 'interchange' turns, probably the 2.35pm Plymouth Friary to Exeter Central in the early 1950s. This engine has been fitted with a larger boiler and 'elbow' outside steampipes. Mike Daly

Standing at the head of an up express at Plymouth North Road on an unrecorded date, but probably in the 1920s, is 4059 'PRINCESS PATRICIA'. The buildings in the left background were in the Engineers' yard.

Heading a down stopping train formed of clerestory stock, at Dawlish, is 4063 'BATH ABBEY'. This engine was one of ten 'Abbeys' which were rebuilt as 'Castles'. A.G. Ellis

7

SAINT CLASS AND OTHER GWR 4-6-0s

The earlier 'Saints' entered service a few years before the 'Stars', but later, construction of both types was concurrent. The second member of the class was converted to a 4-4-2 and thirteen more were built with that wheel arrangement. As with No.40, this was to carry out comparisons with the De Glehn compounds. They were converted to 4-6-0s between April 1912 and January 1913 and worked many of the principal express's, being capable of remarkably high speeds. Indeed, one of the class, 2905 'LADY MACBETH', was credited with attaining at least 120mph when just released from the works and on a trial run 'light engine' from Stoke Gifford to Swindon. Thirty-nine of the class lasted into the BR period.

This is 100 'WILLIAM DEAN', the first member of the 'Saint' class, that appeared in February 1902, at the throat of the shed yard at Laira, with the crew proudly posing for the photographer. It had been named 'DEAN' until November 1902. From the end of 1912 it was renumbered to become 2900. This engine differed from later 'Saints' in having its nameplate on the front splasher, instead of on the centre one, and it also had higher set frames and other detail differences.

A down express hauled by 100 'WILLIAM DEAN' emerges from Parsons tunnel heading for Teignmouth. As the line is single this indicates that the picture was taken before 4 June 1905. The deep front buffer beam is apparent.
A.G. Ellis

Waiting to depart from Plymouth North Road with an up express on 8 August 1925 is Saint class 2904 'LADY GODIVA'.

In the yard outside Laira shed, on an unspecified date, is 2912 'SAINT AMBROSE'. The interesting point of this photo is that the engine is fitted with an eight wheeled tender. This was originally attached to the GWRs' only Pacific, 111 'THE GREAT BEAR' which marks the date as being in the early 1930s, as after April 1931 as the engine had been fitted with outside steampipes. It also has curved drop ends. Rail Archive Stephenson/Photomatic

An up stopping train standing at Brent is in the charge of 'Saint' class 172 QUICKSILVER during it's period as a 4-4-2, which places it between 1905 and March 1907 when it was re-named 'THE ABBOT' and became 2972. A.G. Ellis

'SAINTS' ON PARADE IN LAIRA SHED YARD

This engine, 173 'ROBINS BOLITHO', that was always a 4-6-0, was built in March 1905. As a Locomotive Inspector is on the engine it is probable that it was brand new and on test; it later became 2973.

Here is 175 prior to 1907, as it not named. As it looks brand new the date is probably 1905. Later, this engine carried three names which, in succession, were 'VISCOUNT CHURCHILL' from 1907, 'SIR ERNEST PALMER' from February 1924 and 'LORD PALMER' from October 1933. The author saw the engine carrying the last name in the late 1930s, when it was shedded at Newton Abbot. It had been re-numbered 2975.

'SAINTS' ON PARADE IN LAIRA SHED YARD

Now we see 176, also un-named, which dates the photo as pre April 1907 when it was named 'WINTERSTOKE'. It later became 2976.

Here is 178 'KIRKLAND'. The engine became 2978, being re-named 'CHARLES. J. HAMBRO' in May 1935.

To end this group at Laira we see 180, un-named and running as a 4-4-2. In March 1907 it was named 'COUER DE LION' and later became 2980.

In the yard at Millbay shed is 'Saint' 185 'PEVERIL OF THE PEAK' as a 4-4-2. This name dates the shot as after April 1907, because prior to that date it carried the name 'WINTERSTOKE'. This was prior to August 1912 when the engine became a 4-6-0, and it became 2985.

'Saint' 187 'BRIDE OF LAMMERMOOR' as a 4-4-2 at Dawlish with a down express. As the engine was named 'ROBERTSON' between November 1905 and April 1907, this narrows down the date the photo was taken. It was later re-numbered 2987. The author recalls seeing this engine, which was shedded at Banbury at the time, in a filthy condition, pounding up St Austell bank in June 1945 at the head of a long passenger train.

The crew are posing on 'Saint' 98 at Laira shed, pre March 1907, when it was named 'VANGUARD'. In December of the same year it became 'ERNEST CUNARD' and later became 2998.

A view of the other side of 98 at Laira, for the benefit of modellers. The Locomotive Inspector, featured in photo 74, is present on the engine. He must have been based at Laira.

This was a rarity on the GWR, being the sole member built of its class. 4-6-0 36 was designed by Dean and entered service in August 1896. It was nicknamed 'The Crocodile', and was designed to work trains through the Severn tunnel. It performed this task successfully but the design was not perpetuated. It was withdrawn at the end of 1905 and is seen at a location that resembles the west end of Newton Abbot, with the end of the wagon works behind the loco.

This view of Laira shed yard on 31 March 1963 contains three withdrawn 'County' class 4-6-0s. All had been fitted with double chimneys but had lost their name and numberplates. From left to right they are 1003 'COUNTY OF WILTS', 1015 'COUNTY OF GLOUCESTER' and 1004 'COUNTY OF SOMERSET'. Maurice Dart

8

OTHER 4-6-0s

For a time a 'Navy Week' used to be held at Devonport. For the 1934 event, held in August, an extra special attraction was provided by the presence of SR 'Lord Nelson' class 859 'LORD HOOD', which was placed on display at Devonport SR station. As this class of engines was not permitted to work over the SR route west of Exeter, the engine had to use the GWR line from Exeter St Davids to Plymouth North Road, where it is seen on arrival. The engine was stationed at Stewarts Lane, Battersea, at that time. Russel Leitch

Following the formation of British Railways in 1948 a series of trials were carried out to assess the performance of a variety of locomotives at work in areas different from their normal stamping grounds. LMS 'BLACK FIVE' 45253 from Kentish Town shed, London, waits to depart from Plymouth North Road with an up trial run on 6 July 1948. Stephenson Locomotive Society

At the head of another trial run at Plymouth North Road on 7 July 1948, is LNER B1 class 61251 which was shedded at Kings Cross. The GWR dynamometer car is behind the engine, which later was named 'OLIVER BURY'. Stephenson Locomotive Society

A very unusual visitor on an up Goods at Bere Alston in the early 1960s was a very grubby BR Standard class 5, 73115 'KING PELLINMORE' from Nine Elms shed, which, presumably, had been 'borrowed' by Exmouth Junction to work this duty. Mike Daly

Another rare visitor, from Shrewsbury shed in August 1958, was Standard class 5, 73133 which was fitted with Caprotti valve gear. It is backing on to Newton Abbot shed having come off a down train. Mike Daly

Exmouth Junction gained some Standard class 5s towards the end of steam working in Devon. One of these, 73166, brings an up goods into Devonport Kings Road in 1964. The signal box can be seen above the wagons. The leading two wagons are Conflats carrying tanks, the third vehicle is a Shock open and the next three are Palbricks.

One of Exmouth Junction's BR Standard class 4s, 75025, brings an up goods through Devonport Kings Road in 1964.

9

2-6-4 TANKS

For just over three months in 1951-52, Exmouth Junction shed received three LMS Fairburn 4MT 2-6-4Ts. These were to be tried out as possible replacements for N class 2-6-0s. One of them, 42103, heads a down passenger from Exeter Central towards St Budeaux Victoria Road. The picture has been taken partly against the light. Mike Daly

After Laira had lost its steam allocation, some embarrassment was felt at times when Exmouth Junction continued to send steam locos down to Plymouth hauling trains on the SR route. A grubby BR Standard class 4 2-6-4T, 80037 is standing at Plymouth station in 1964.

10

GWR SMALL PRAIRIE TANKS

These popular and useful engines comprised three classes. First there were the eleven members of the 4400 class which had wheels of 4ft 1½ inch diameter. These were followed by the seventy-five members of the 4500 class fitted with driving wheels of 4ft 7½ inch diameter and side tanks which held 1000 gallons. These were usually called 'small tank 45s'. The third batch was the 4575 class which differed from the 4500s by being fitted with tanks of 1300 gallon capacity and were known as 'large tank 45s'. These classes worked trains on most of the branch lines in the West Country.

We start this section with a batch of 'small tank 45s,' of which 4502 is alongside the coal stack, by the coaler, at Newton Abbot shed between April 1926 and January 1929. A.G.Ellis

The first thirty of these engines were originally numbered in the 21XX series. Here is 2169, which became 4508, on a down passenger at Torre in 'as built' condition. The date is between June 1907 and early 1909 as the engine retains its small bunker and has its numberplate on the side of the tank. The vehicle behind the engine appears to be a GWR Hounds van.

Locomotive Club of Great Britain/Ken Nunn collection

Bringing a local down goods into Plymouth North Road between 1937 and 1940 is 4509. Two refuge sidings are on the right.

Still retaining a small bunker, but fitted with front end struts, is 4516 which is in the yard at Newton Abbot shed. Note the mark on the side of the tank where the original number of 2177 was carried.

Around 1950 these locos were used to work stopping trains from Plymouth Friary to Tavistock over the SR route. Taken against the light is 4518, from Laira shed, north of St Budeaux Victoria Road. Mike Daly

A photo taken at Brent between 1911 and 1912 has 2185 taking water as the crew pose. This engine, from Newton Abbot shed, was in the first batch which had their numberplates placed on the side of the bunker; it became 4524.

A train of mainly clerestory empty stock, probably bound for Millbay and hauled by 4523, is between Lipson Vale and Mannamead on 14 May 1925. Pamlin Prints

On a train of empty ballast wagons at Marsh Mills in the 1930s is 4529. The industrial premises in the background were served by a siding.

A train from the Launceston branch hauled by Laira's 4531 has just arrived at Plymouth North Road's platforms 2 and 3 in the 1930s.

During July 1919, 4550 is stopped at Teignmouth with an up stopping train to Exeter St Davids, composed of an assortment of carriages. The stock is wearing the crimson lake livery. Note the centrally pivoted up starting signal. The 'BUCHANAN'S SCOTCH WHISKY' sign is prominently displayed on the stone wall. A.G. Ellis

In October 1951, 'Large tank 45' 4582 from Newton Abbot shed is shunting goods wagons at Totnes. The wooden goods shed is prominent.

This photo shows the author placing a wreath on the smokebox door of Laira's 5568 whilst the engine takes water at Plymouth station at 7.28pm on 29 December 1962. This was the 6.20pm to Launceston which actually departed at 7.32pm on the last day of service, hence the 'Funeral Rights'. Owing to blizzard conditions, which blocked routes and froze points, the train reached Tavistock, at 12.20am and terminated there.

The next group of photos cover the small wheeled 4400 class, which were originally numbered in the 31XX series until late in 1912. Shortly after arrival at Kingsbridge on 23 July 1910 is 3101, which later became 4401. The numberplate is still on the side of the tank. The loco was shedded at Laira at this time. Locomotive Club of Great Britain/Ken Nunn collection

Most of Laira's 44s spent some time sub-shedded at Princetown to work the steeply graded and sharply curved branch line from Yelverton. Two experiments were carried out to ease the wear on wheel flanges caused by the banked sharp curves. The engine concerned was 4402 which has the later equipment fitted. It is coupling up ready to take the train to Princetown in the late 1930s. Stephenson Locomotive Society

Old faithful 4402 suffered a 'mishap' (the GWR never had 'accidents') at Yelverton on 25 January 1939, following a shunting movement to run around the train. The engine had propelled the carriages out past the point for the shunting neck, reversed a few yards and run forward into the shunting neck, to permit the carriage(s) to gravitate back into the platform, after which it ran back and coupled up. However, the signalman had not reset the points, and the train departed before the signal had been cleared. It accelerated up the shunting neck with the depicted result, completely demolishing a wooden hut. The engine was taken to Laira, from where it went to Swindon works. Following repairs it returned to Princetown on 8 May in the same year. Great Western Railway

These two locos in the yard at Laira shed, in the late 1920s, are a modellers' and railway historians' delight. At the rear is ex Cornwall Minerals Railway 0-6-0 ST 1398, with 4405 at the front. The top of the locomotive hoist can be seen behind the locos, with one vehicle of the breakdown train to the right.

Shunting is being carried out at Princetown by 4403, probably in the late 1920s. This scene includes the signal box, station building and goods shed, with the solitary clerestory passenger coach at the platform and a large goods van on the run round loop. At 1373 ft above sea level, this desolate location could claim to be the highest station on the GWR.

This broadside view of 4408 in Laira shed yard, taken between 1928 and 1930, shows the rear extension to accommodate the enlarged bunker. Part of the platform of Laira Halt can be seen above the engine. A.G. Ellis

Viewed from the other side, 4409 is under repair at Laira in almost the same spot as the previous view. The coupling, connecting and piston rods have been removed from the engine. It was taken late in 1927 or in 1928. A.G. Ellis

11

GWR LARGE PRAIRIE, LMS AND STANDARD 2-6-2Ts

These large GWR tanks have been prominent in the area for many years, as they have been used to provide assistance to trains over the South Devon banks. They were regularly used on stopping trains between Exeter St Davids and Kingswear. LMS Ivatt 2-6-2Ts appeared in the 1950s on the Southern Region at Plymouth to work local services and trains on the Callington branch. BR Standard 3MT 2-6-2Ts arrived at Newton Abbot for a short stay in 1956, but many worked from Exmouth Junction in the BR period.

One of the first type of large Prairies to be used for assisting trains was the 3150 class, and 3156 is in the yard at Newton Abbot shed, with a crew member posing during May 1923. A.G. Ellis

A very similar type was the old 3100 class that later became the 5100 class. Ready for duty in the yard at Newton Abbot shed in the 1920s is 3129, which became 5129. A.G. Ellis

Pausing in the up platform at Totnes between banking duty, target No.2 is 5132, probably in the mid 1940s. The author saw this engine on banking duty at this location in 1945.

About 1946 Laira swapped 5101 class 5172 for Taunton's 5100 class 5148. This engine went on to become the last member of its class, regularly performing banking duties on Hemerdon. It is in Laira shed yard in September 1949. The loco's crew, together a shed disposal man on 8750 class 0-6-0PT 4656, pose for the camera. Maurice Dart

The 5101 class was a development of the 5100 class. This scene, taken on a wet day at Heathfield, has Newton Abbot shed's 4109 running in on a train from Moretonhampstead, the longest station name on the GWR, on 4 January 1958. It was taken from a train to that location, hauled by a 4800 class 0-4-2T. A Teign valley train hauled by a 4575 class 2-6-2T is waiting in the bay platform. H.B. Priestley

On 19 May 1957 a special train was worked to Kingswear by preserved 4-4-0 3440 'CITY OF TRURO'. From Newton Abbot, that shed's 5101 class 4179 provided assistance. The train, with the author on board, is passing Kingkerswell.

This is an unusual sighting of an Engineer's train using the wartime connection from St Budeaux Victoria Road to St Budeaux East in the mid-1950s on an overcast day. It is hauled by Laira's 5101 class 5175. The carriages on the right are in the SR yard. Mike Daly

Late in 1959 Laira received a member of a type that was new to the shed. A member of the 6100 class, a later development of the large Prairies, was 6166, which is in the shed yard on 21 February 1960. This class was mainly employed to work suburban services from London to Reading, Oxford and Aylesbury. Maurice Dart

A pair of LMS Ivatt 2MT 2-6-2Ts are at Bere Alston late in 1961. Plymouth Friary's 41315 is shunting the yard, as 41238 from Exmouth Junction shed waits to depart with a train to Callington.

Newton Abbot shed was host to three 2-6-2Ts on 13 May 1956. Two are BR 3MTs 82006 and 82033 with ex-works 'small tank 45' 4561 at the rear. This last engine has been preserved. The SC below the 83A shedplate on 82033 denotes that the loco is fitted with a self cleaning smokebox. Maurice Dart

MOGUL 2-6-0s

These mixed traffic types were used widely by both the GWR and SR in the area for working local passenger and goods trains for many years. They were good reliable engines. In early days the GWR used the Dean designed outside framed 'Aberdare' class, which were superceded by 4300 class Moguls. The SR used N class together with a few U class. For two short periods some three cylinder U1s were tried unsuccessfully and the author once saw an N1 in the area. Latterly, some unusual visitors appeared infrequently.

GWR Moguls worked the interchange turns over the SR route between Plymouth and Exeter fairly regularly. One of them, a very clean 5376 from Laira shed, approaches St Budeaux Victoria Road with an up passenger to Exeter Central on 17 March 1956. Mike Daly

Taken about 1922 whilst stopped at Torquay with a down express is Mogul 5346 from Newton Abbot shed. Locomotive Club of Great Britain/Ken Nunn collection

This photographically imperfect photo is reproduced because it records an extremely unusual occurrence on 13 December 1953. On that day the GWR main line was blocked east of Totnes by wagons which had broken away from a train on Dainton bank and had subsequently become derailed, so all GWR trains were diverted to run over the SR route by reversing direction at North Road. However, a 'leave' special to Birmingham departed from Admiralty Platform, sited within the Royal Naval Barracks, and used the wartime connection from St Budeaux East to gain SR metals. The thirteen coach train is on the connection on that bitterly cold morning hauled by Moguls 6319 from Laira and 5339 from Newton Abbot, both exerting maximum effort to keep the heavy train moving. The author was in trouble for arriving home late that day for his Sunday dinner, but he could not have missed that opportunity! Maurice Dart

Some of the Moguls numbered in the 53XX series were modified by fitting additional weight to the front end to give increased adhesion on curved sections of track. The routes in Devon and Cornwall abound with curves, so naturally many of the modified locos were to be found working in the area. They were re-numbered in the 83XX series and 8314 is passing Laira Halt with a down express in 1937. The 83s were later converted back and regained their original numbers.

'Aberdare' class 2601 enters Plymouth North Road, past the wooden built Parcels Office with an up goods, probably from Millbay, before September 1936, when the loco was withdrawn from service.

A view inside the roundhouse at Laira on 15 June 1926 shows 'Aberdare' 2620 stabled. This engine was shedded at St Blazey in 1922.   H.C. Casserley

A very clean 'Aberdare' 2651, is entering North Road with a down ballast train during 1914.

The driver of Laira 'Aberdare' 2658 watches the photographer whilst stopped at North Road on 7 August 1923.

A very clean 'Aberdare', 2676, probably ex works, is in Newton Abbot shed yard in the 1920s.

The first SR N class 2-6-0 to reach Plymouth was 831 which later became 1831. It must have had some problems as it went to Friary shed, where it is under the hoist on 8 August 1924, with two sets of its driving wheels removed. Behind it, also with it's driving wheels removed, is 0-6-2T 758 'LORD ST LEVAN', which normally worked on the Callington branch.
Stephenson Locomotive Society

The U class 2-6-0s had larger diameter driving wheels than the Ns, which is shown by the presence of splashers over them on 31794, seen north of St Budeaux Victoria Road on an up passenger to Exeter Central in the 1950s. This engine was an unusual visitor to Plymouth as it was shedded at Yeovil. Mike Daly

A few U1s were tried out briefly in the late 1930s and again in the early 1960s. Their outside cylinders were of a different design to those on the Us and the front end was much deeper to accommodate the inside cylinder. These differences are shown to good effect in this view of 1900 on the turntable at Friary shed in the summer of 1937. Stephenson Locomotive Society

Swindon Works built some BR Standard 3MT 2-6-0s, and a couple of them, at least, worked down to Plymouth whilst running in. On 16 April 1954 the author found 77006 on shed at Laira. The loco was later allocated to Hamilton shed near Glasgow. The previous day, unknown to me, 77005 had arrived. Maurice Dart

Surprisingly, in 1953 three newly built LMS type Ivatt class 2MT 2-6-0s were allocated to ex GWR sheds at Bristol. One of these was 46526 from St Phillips Marsh which being coaled at Laira in April 1953. The author happened to be passing North Road on his bicycle as the engine backed out to Laira, so he took the only possible course of action and chased it out there. Next in line is 4-6-0 6009 'KING CHARLES II' from Old Oak Common shed which had worked in on the down 'Limited'. Note the piles of ash that has been removed from the smokeboxes of engines. Maurice Dart

SOUTHERN 0-6-2 TANKS

Apart from the pair from the Plymouth, Devonport & South Western Junction Railway, only a few of the E1/R class were seen at Plymouth after they had been displaced from the Halwill to Torrington line by LMS Ivatt 2-6-2Ts.

A pre 1922 photo has 757 'EARL OF MOUNT EDGCUMBE' in LSWR livery, at Bere Alston on a passenger train for Callington. Stephenson Locomotive Society

Here a rather grubby 757 'EARL OF MOUNT EDGCUMBE' shunts the yard at Bere Alston, probably around 1946. The engine is in wartime SR livery.

The other ex PDSWJ engine, 'LORD ST LEVAN', now renumbered to 30758, is on pilot duty at Friary shed shunting coal wagons in the early 1950s. The engine had recently returned from a visit to Eastleigh Works. Mike Daly

One of the E1/R class 0-6-2Ts, 32095, is shunting the yard at St.Budeaux Victoria Road in 1955 or 1956. Mike Daly

14

0-6-0 TENDER ENGINES

Photographs of GWR 0-6-0s in the area are hard to locate, as even the 2251 class were very infrequent visitors west of Exeter. One was reputed to have been allocated to Laira during the early 1950s, but that was probably a mis-entry as the engine in question never appeared there. The older 'Dean Goods' had been displaced by the arrival of Moguls in the years before and after 1920. The Southern occasionally used 0-6-0s to work goods, but not so much after the N class 2-6-0s arrived in the mid-1920s.

A rare visitor to Kingswear, where it is shunting goods wagons during September 1956, was 2251 class 2293 from Swindon shed. Judging from its external condition the engine has recently emerged from a visit to Newton Abbot works, which would explain its unusual presence in the area. A.G. Ellis

One of the later batch of 2251 class 0-6-0s was 3215 from St Phillips Marsh shed, which is awaiting coaling at Laira in the late 1950s. Mike Steer

Having purchased this imperfect and damaged photo of a 'Dean Goods' at Laira, taken in 1919 or 1920, it has presented many of my railway enthusiast colleagues and myself with queries. Firstly, there is no numberplate on the engine. This most certainly means that it is one of the engines that was taken over by the War Department in the First World War for duties abroad, and had been returned following the end of hostilities. But all of those were reputed to have had a painted on number applied. Now, by very carefully pouring over the photo, it seems as if there could be the number 2549 painted very faintly on the cab side. It is a distinct possibility as that engine saw service with the War Department and as it has a 'fluted' coupling rod, it has to be one of the batch numbered between 2511 and 2580. The other query is, what was it doing at Laira, as none of the returned engines were shedded anywhere near Plymouth. So, over to you, the readers.

This veteran 'Standard Goods' was constructed in March 1868 and lasted for many years. It ended its days based at Exeter and is seen at Plymouth North Road running tender first with an up goods on 8 September 1928. The engine was withdrawn from service in February 1930.

We start looking at SR 0-6-0s with another veteran that dates from May 1878. Alongside the loco shed at Devonport is single-framed LSWR 'Beyer Goods' 371. Despite their class name these locos handled a fair amount of light passenger work in the West Country during the early 1900s, which roughly dates this photo. At the start of the First World War this engine was in use at Guildford, but during the middle of 1917 it was laid aside at Eastleigh where some parts were removed from it and these were used to keep other members of the class operating. It was finally withdrawn from service during April 1922.

The crew on LSWR 0395 class 0-6-0 83 pose alongside the engine shed at Devonport. This engine started life in November 1885 numbered 69 and became 83 in March 1889. In the SR system it became 3083 and in BR days it was renumbered again to 30565, and lasted until February 1953.

One of the 0395 class, which spent almost all of its life in the West Country was LSWR 29, seen at Bere Alston on a passenger train standing at the Callington branch platform in the mid-1920s. From the early 1900s these engines were placed on the 'Duplicate List' and gained a 0 in front of their number, hence the number carried being 029. It was renumbered by BR to 30564 and survived until April 1958.

Here is the same engine, now numbered 30564, shunting a down goods at Devonport King's Road during 1955.   Mike Daly

The other type of 0-6-0 seen on the SR in Devon, was the 700 class that were nicknamed 'Black Motors'. This loco, which is outside Friary shed in the early 1920s, started life numbered 713 but became 352 in mid-1898.

15

0-6-0 TANK ENGINES

This section is one of the largest in this book, due to the GWR adopting this type of engine for general shunting duties, empty stock movements and transfer goods, along with branch and light main line passenger duties. To cater for the variety of tasks performed, numerous variants based on the standard design, were produced. The earlier engines were built as saddle tanks, but from the early 1900s all newly constructed engines were fitted with pannier tanks. Quite a number of the older types are included but I have avoided going into masses of technical detail to point out the differences in the classes. Some batches were built for the GWR by outside contractors and later engines were fitted with redesigned cabs. One batch was only fitted with a steam brake and three link couplings. These were mainly used for shunting at docks in South Wales, with a few at Swindon as pilots for the Locomotive Carriage and Wagon works. Many of the saddle tanks were converted to pannier tanks over the years. Any mention of the GWR immediately brings to one's mind the image of a 'pannier'. The total number built reached 2393 and all except 21 of them had inside cylinders. For a while, in the 1940s, they were fittingly nicknamed 'Matchboxes'. The use of 0-6-0Ts by the SR in the area was minimal.

One of the 5700 class, which was fitted with the older type of cab, was 8709. It is alongside the works at Newton Abbot on the line leading to the coaler on 24 August 1933. This became the standard design, fitted with driving wheels of 4ft 7½ inch diameter, until the advent of the later 9400 class.

Later locos of this type, fitted with redesigned cabs, were designated the 8750 class, and a pair of Laira's allocation are 3629 on the coaler ramp and 3639 on one of the shed yard outlet lines. Mike Steer

A most unusual sight on 9 August 1958 was that of two of Laira's 8750 class locos, 3629 and 4653, in store outside the SR shed at Friary. Mike Daly

A train of parcels and other vans enters Plymouth North Road, probably bound for Millbay, on 3 November 1958. Running bunker first is 4575 class 2-6-2T 5551 from St Blazey and the pilot loco is Laira's 8750 class 3686. The author once watched this pannier very slowly bring a 'Transfer' goods train of 92 empty wagons and vans plus a brake van into Laira yard from Tavistock Junction yard. When it finally stopped, the Brake van was opposite Laira Junction signal box and the engine was outside Mount Gould Junction signal box. As the distance between the boxes was 37 chains, that train was about 66 yards short of a being a half mile long! Not bad for a 'pannier'.

Despite becoming British Railways on 1 January 1948 a few engines continued to carry their old livery for years afterwards. An example of this is Laira's 8750 class 4658 still lettered GWR at Plymouth North Road on 15 May 1958.

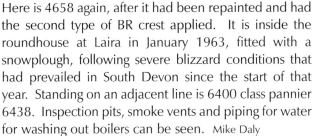

Here is 4658 again, after it had been repainted and had the second type of BR crest applied. It is inside the roundhouse at Laira in January 1963, fitted with a snowplough, following severe blizzard conditions that had prevailed in South Devon since the start of that year. Standing on an adjacent line is 6400 class pannier 6438. Inspection pits, smoke vents and piping for water for washing out boilers can be seen. Mike Daly

Something very unusual occurred in 1961 when Laira received withdrawn 8750 class 6771, which had resided at Cardiff East dock shed. The 67s had never worked in the West Country as they were the batch that were only fitted with a steam brake, so were not permitted to work over main lines, being purely shunting engines. Early in 1962 it is inside the Laira roundhouse where it was used as a stationary boiler to generate steam. Two inspection pits occupy the foreground and 4500 class 2-6-2T 4567 is in the background. Mike Daly

A requirement to replace older pannier tank locos used on light passenger work was met by fitting the standard type of pannier tank with a boiler of lower pressure. First came the Auto fitted 5400 class of which only 5412 was at Laira. The next development was the Auto fitted 6400 class that had boilers of 165lb pressure compared to the 200lb of the 8750 class. Laira received several of these and used them on the "Saltash Motors" as they were locally known. One was also employed, at times, as 'station pilot' at North Road. This photo, which was taken completely against the light in the 1950s, shows pilot 6406, still lettered GWR. It has just derailed at the east end of North Road, after backing through a catch point, against a ground signal that was set at danger. This particular set of points claimed a 'Grange' class 4-6-0 in similar circumstances in the late 1950s, part way through a summer Saturday afternoon. The author saw the aftermath but, alas, he did not have a camera with him at the time. Mike Daly

Now we have a photo of a 64 taken at Ashburton in the early days of preservation on the Dart Valley Railway. A special train, chartered by the Locomotive Club of Great Britain, is departing from the station for Totnes hauled by 6412 on 24 October 1968. This was in the all too brief period when through running from British Railways at Totnes was permitted and the railway extended the full length of the original branch line to Ashburton.

Still in its GWR livery at Laira shed during June 1949 is 6400 class 6421. This engine had yet to be fitted with a 'Top Feed'. A train of vans occupies the down slow line and a train is signalled on the up main.

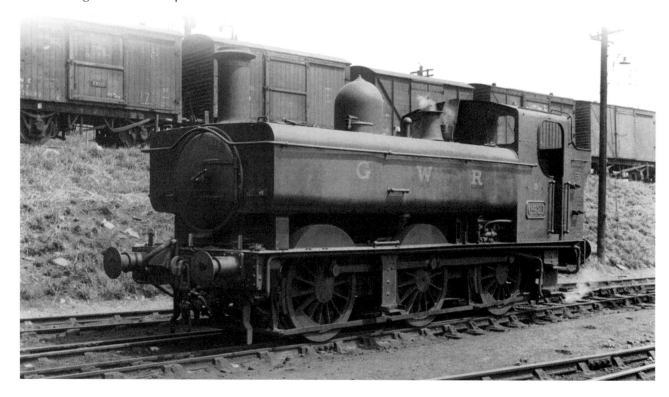

An unidentified member of Laira's 64s takes a typical 'Saltash Motor formation out of North Road to Laira, in the late 1950s. In the working timetable these were described as 'Auto' trains, but they were announced at North Road as 'Railcars'. Just to confuse things even more the general public called them 'Motor trains'. So 'take your pick'. During quiet periods a two coach formation, usually at the rear of the engine, was used, but for the rush hours '64 Sandwiches' were used. Mike Daly

The 7400 class was a batch of engines with a boiler pressure of 180lb. They were not fitted for working Auto trains but could be used on light passenger or goods trains, or on pilot work. Engaged on the latter duty at North Road on 23 July 1938 is 7422 which, together with 7427, was allocated to Laira at that time. This engine has the 'GWR Roundel' on its tank. A.G. Ellis

Here is 7422 again, but this time it is shunting carriages at Newton Abbot on 30 August 1945 and has been repainted with GWR on its tanks. The vehicle in the background to the left of the engine is a Syphon H van.
H.C.Casserley

From 1947, the GWR further developed the 'pannier' with the building of the 9400 class. These were fitted with a coned boiler having a pressure of 200lb. This interesting photo, from the mid 1950s, shows Laira's 8422 working the down 'St Blazey goods' past St Budeaux East running on the up line. 'Gangers' (PW men) are working on the down line, on which a cracked rail had been found on the points at the junction with the branch line to Bullpoint, which can be glimpsed diverging right. The SR main line to Devonport and Plymouth is upper left, on which the rather obscure Weston Mill Halt was in the cutting just before the overline bridge.   Mike Daly

One day in the early 1960s, one of the new diesel multiple units was unavailable, and neither was one of Laira's few remaining 6400s, so 8422 was used to work with an 'Auto -car' set in 'non-Auto' mode, on the 'Saltash Motor'. It has just passed St Budeaux East heading for Camels Head viaduct. Mike Daly

Also from 1949, A new 1600 class lightweight pannier, retaining wheels of 4ft 1½ in diameter entered service. These were to replace older panniers with small wheels which were used on sharply curved, lightly laid lines, such as in dock areas or on some country branch lines. Laira and Newton Abbot each had one of these engines and 1650 has come on to the coaling line at Laira shed on 6 April 1957. When not working on the Sutton Harbour line, it was usually to be found hidden away, resting inside the roundhouse.

The direct predecessors of the 5700 class were the 2721 class, which itself possessed variants described as the 2779 and 2796 classes. 'Half cab' 2785 has arrived at Totnes on an unknown date before 1923, with a goods from Ashburton. Note the original Brunel overall roofs.

The engine featured in the previous photo, 2785, turned out to be long-lived, and unfortunately suffered damage during a German air raid. It is seen after the raid at Newton Abbot on 20 August 1940. Several nearby engines in the shed yard were also damaged. However 2785 was repaired and survived until April 1948.

Now we have an example of a 2021 class engine running as a saddle tank on 8 November 1924. 2050, fitted with a domeless boiler, is working a 'Transfer goods' from Tavistock Junction, past Crabtree, bound for Laira yard. Stephenson Locomotive Society

Some members of the 2021 class gained full cabs and, of course, were fitted with pannier tanks. At an unknown date, but pre 1939, 2097 is inside the roundhouse at Laira.

Here is another 2021 class variation as 2116 shunts goods wagons at Marsh Mills in the 1920s. It has a 'Half–cab', but is fitted with a 'Backplate' on the bunker.

Next we will see some members of the older 850 and similar 1901 class engines. On 1 August 1925, fully modernised 1927 shunts at North Road. Notice the well defined H section spokes on the wheels of the locomotive which was withdrawn during October 1929. Stephenson Locomotive Society

Another of the same class brings a goods from Laira yard for the Sutton Harbour line past Friary Junction on 30 May 1925. 'Half-cab' 1930 remained in Devon and Cornwall and went on to survive until August 1949. Stephenson Locomotive Society.

A member of the class with a 'Half-cab' and saddle tank, 1932, stands in Laira yard as the crew and the shunter pose in the 1920s. This engine lasted until April 1930. The chalked inscription on the shunting truck reads "Flying Prince, National" so presumably a horse of that name was a possible winner in that event! Stephenson Locomotive Society

Standing on a non-platform line with passenger stock at North Road in 1923, retaining a 'Half-cab' and saddle tank is 1941. After rebuilding this engine lasted until February 1951. Stephenson Locomotive Society

In the shed yard at Laira on 15 June 1926 is 1952, another fully modernised member of the class which worked until November 1928.   H.C.Casserley

In March 1912, in the yard at Millbay shed, is very clean 1901 class 1973 running as a 0-4-2 ST. The coupling rods have been removed from the rear driving wheels to assist in negotiating sharp curves in Millbay Docks. This engine was shedded at Laira when withdrawn in December 1949.

At the throat of Laira shed yard during 1932 is 1993. There appears to be a caricature of Mickey Mouse on the side of the bunker. The author saw this engine as it survived until April 1951 at Barry shed. Stephenson Locomotive Society

Shunting at Plymouth Millbay on a very wet day in the early 1920s is 1999. The crew have unrolled the 'weather sheet' and fastened it down in an attempt to provide some shelter to the 'Half-cab'. After modernising this engine lasted until June 1946, and was seen by the author at Exeter. A.G.Ellis

One of the very early members of the 850 class was 863, which is at North Road on pilot duty sometime in the early 1920s. After gaining pannier tanks it survived until May 1932. The hoardings contain some interesting advertisements. Stephenson Locomotive Society

Now we come to a member of the 1854 class. These were fitted with driving wheels of 4 ft 6 in diameter. A grubby 1729 is in the works yard at Newton Abbot on 24 July 1930 hiding a breakdown crane. This engine was withdrawn in September 1942 following damage sustained at Castle Cary during an air raid.   A.G.Ellis

Here is 1736, in the works yard at Newton Abbot on 15 July 1936, with the driver posing as the loco is coupled to a crane. This engine lasted until April 1945.

With another driver posing, we have 1797 on the coaling line at Newton Abbot shed, also on 15 July 1936. The author saw this engine at St Austell many times during 1944 and 1945. It was withdrawn during the following year.
Ken Davies

Another member of the 1854 class, 1876, is pilot at North Road during July 1929. This specimen lasted until February 1936. Stephenson Locomotive Society

An engine that survived until January 1949 was 1897 which is passing Crabtree on 6 August 1925 with a goods from the Launceston branch bound for Laira yard. The train contains an assortment of pre-grouping companies' vehicles. Stephenson Locomotive Society

Earlier GWR six coupled tanks were the outside–framed 1076 or 'Buffalo'class. They started as saddle tanks but most gained pannier tanks before being withdrawn from service. With their 4 ft 7½ in diameter driving wheels they were really the very first predecessors of the 5700 class. Around 1930, one of them, a very clean 1148, is piloting tender first running 'Star' class 4 - 6 - 0 4048 'PRINCESS VICTORIA' on a Newton Abbot to Paignton local passenger near Aller Junction. W.Potter

'Buffalo' class 1235 is climbing the bank to Mannamead and has passed Lipson Junction with an 'Auto' train for Millbay on 14 May 1925.

With clerestory stock in tow during 1935, 'Buffalo' class 1271 has arrived at Tavistock and is taking water. The fireman is astride the top of the engine, which has gained a full cab.

A 'Full-cab' member of the 'Buffalo' class, 1600, has reached Plympton with a four coach 'Auto Sandwich' in the early 1930s. One of the Auto coaches can be identified as 74. The engine has just completed taking water, and the train will need to use a cross-over and shunt to the down platform to return to Plymouth. The station and platforms have now disappeared but the large properties in the background remain, unaltered.

A team of 'gangers' pause in their work and several of them watch the progress of 'Buffalo' class 1286 as it passes with a down goods west of Brent on 3 August 1925. The train contains three ex London & North Western Railway vehicles.   Stephenson Locomotive Society

Whereas all of types of GWR 0-6-0Ts have so far, possessed inside cylinders, the next types have outside cylinders and short wheelbases for use on sharply curved mineral lines or at docks. There were five members in the 1361 class of 0-6-0 saddle tanks, which was based on an ex Cornwall Minerals Railway design that had been rebuilt by the GWR from an original side tank version. All of the class were originally based at Plymouth or at St Blazey. Here is 1361 at rest inside Laira's roundhouse in the late 1930s. P. Ransome-Wallis

The next member of the class, 1362, is near the coaler at Laira shed in August 1937.

The most well known member of the class, 1363, is preserved at the Great Western Society's depot at Didcot. It is seen here shunting at Millbay docks on a damp and murky 9 August 1952. Mike Daly

The publisher suggested that I include this very early attempt for sentiment. I tried to record 1364 at Laira, when I was learning to use a camera, one evening towards the end of September 1947. The result is a silhouette of the loco standing at the foot of the coaler ramp. I was using an old box camera with a 'push over' shutter lever, and one of the viewfinders showed a double image! Maurice Dart

At times there was one member of the class resident at Newton Abbot to shunt the works area. However, taken in the BR period, 1364 is outside the works awaiting a visit. Note the facsimile outline of a GWR 4-2-2 locomotive at the top of the weather vane on the roof of the locomotive works.

Taken before 1939 at Millbay docks, 1365 is carrying out shunting. One of the class was usually housed during the week, in a small shed in the Docks complex. The loco returned to Laira at the weekend for servicing.

The design of the 1361 class was derived from the ex Cornwall Minerals Railway locos, after they had been rebuilt as saddle tanks by the GWR. In the 1920s, shunting at Newton Abbot, is ex CMR 1397 which still retained its 'Half cab'. The driver is watching the photographer. A.G.Ellis

In the yard at Laira shed in the late 1920s is ex CMR 1398, which was the only member of the class to been gain a full cab. This engine had been numbered 1400 until December 1912. The original 1398 had been sold to Sharpness New Docks during April 1883.

This engine started life as London, Brighton & South Coast Railway A1 class 'Terrier' 43 which became 643 and was rebuilt to an A1X class. After becoming SR B643 it was bought by the Weston, Clevedon & Portishead Railway at the end of 1925. It became that railway's No.2 and was named 'PORTISHEAD'. When that line closed completely on 18 May 1940, the GWR purchased two of its locomotives, one of which was this engine that became GWR No.5. They were overhauled and worked in the Bristol area until 1948 when 'PORTISHEAD' was transferred to Taunton, followed by a move to Newton Abbot where this photo was taken on 4 March 1950. It was to be used as a pilot for the shed and works, but stayed for only a couple of months. It still has the shed code TN for Taunton stencilled on the frame but the T has been partly blanked out. The NA code for Newton Abbot had not been applied.

This engine, which has been raised up on blocks to have all of its wheels removed, is alongside Friary shed on 8 November 1924. It is ex Plymouth, Devonport & South Western Junction Railway 'A.S.HARRIS' that became LSWR 756. It ended its days in the London area as pilot at Stewarts Lane shed, Battersea. Stephenson Locomotive Society

Taken between August 1956 and March 1958 is ex LSWR G6 class 30162, which is taking an ex LNER brake van from Laira yard on to the No.2 spur to Cattewater Junction from where it could either run to Cattewater or Turnchapel. It has just crossed the 4 ft 6 in gauge Lee Moor Tramway that ran parallel to the main lines at this location. Mount Gould Junction is in the distance. Mike Daly

16

FRENCH DE GLEHN COMPOUND 4-4-2s

As this type of engine had produced exceptionally good performances when working express passenger trains in France, and was also economical to operate, the GWR most unusually ordered three of them to compare their performance with that of standard GWR locos. They entered service in October 1903 and June 1905 and operated services to the West Country until 1907, when they were then used to work the lines to Wolverhampton and Worcester. Later they were concentrated at Oxford shed.

The first member of the 'Frenchmen' 102 'LA FRANCE' waits at North Road to take over the first up 'Cornish Riviera Limited' on 1 July 1907. This engine always carried a French style longitudinal nameplate on the side of the cab, below its number. In the left background, a 3521 class 4-4-0 waits on a stopping passenger train.   R.Hansford Worth

The Locomotive Inspector, who has been seen in previous photos in this volume, is on the footplate of 102 'LA FRANCE' as it stands at the entrance to the yard at Laira shed in the early 1900s.

The following two engines were somewhat larger than 102. The crew on 104 pose as the engine stands in the same place at Laira as in the previous view, some time between June 1905 and 1907. This engine was named 'ALLIANCE' in 1907 and carried a standard curved GWR nameplate.

BULLDOG CLASS 4-4-0s

This class was a larger boilered version of the Duke class and was prolific in South Devon for a great many years. Many of their names were familiar to the then young author and his parents before the Second World War, as they were regularly seen when travelling to Millbay or to Paignton and Goodrington. The first twenty engines were Dukes rebuilt with new boilers. The class consisted of three main groups, the first of which had curved frames. The second batch was similar, but had straight frames. The last batch of fifteen, that were named after birds, had deeper straight frames. Some of the other visible variations in the class over the years were different types of boilers, and different types of nameplates mounted in different positions on the engines. They handled fast passenger trains until superceded by 4-6-0s, and then worked stopping and branch passenger trains. They later proved excellent assistant engines on the South Devon banks. I make no excuse for including a good batch of photos of these graceful, beautifully proportioned, locomotives, as they constituted part of the everyday railway scene in the area. Along with most of the other GWR 4-4-0s they were involved in the 1912 renumbering scheme.

Ready to take over a down train at Newton Abbot in 1908 is 3282 'MARISTOWE'. This engine had started life as a Duke class and shortly after this picture was taken a corrected nameplate 'MARISTOW' was fitted. It became 3309.

This engine was well known to our family. 3313 *Jupiter* waits in the carriage sidings at Newton Abbot on 17 August 1932. It had originally been a Duke, numbered 3318.   H.R.Norman

One of the older straight framed engines was 3341 *Blasius* which retained an oval combined name and numberplate until it was withdrawn in November 1949. It is working a short Engineer's train west from Newton Abbot and is approaching Aller Junction on 9 July 1947.

The crew are posing on immaculate 3362 'NEWLYN' in the yard at Millbay shed during 1911. The engine became 3350 and its name was removed in July 1930. This happened to several GWR locomotives, as some passengers were thinking that the name on an engine indicated the train's destination.   Mr Pascoe

Retaining its original tender is 3371 'TREGEAGLE' waiting to take over a down train at Plymouth North Road in about 1900. It later became 3359.   Mr Pascoe

Another well known engine to us was 3375 'SIR WATKIN WYNN', which is in Newton Abbot shed yard on 30 August 1947. In the background are 855 class 0-6-0 PT 1760 and 5100 class 2-6-2 T 5113.

Another immaculate engine in Millbay shed yard in 1907 is 3449 Reading. This lost its name, to avoid confusion, during May 1927 having already become 3387.

A silhouette of a Bulldog! This is another of the shots from the first film that I used in the old camera, included for sentiment, at the Publisher's suggestion. Taken against the setting sun, mid-evening in mid-September 1947, 3401 'VANCOUVER' is on the coaling line at Laira shed. A King class 4-6-0 is behind it. The pair had come off a down train at North Road and backed out to the shed.   Maurice Dart

Here is the same engine, viewed from the other side, in the yard at Laira shed in 1932. The author was waiting at Exeter Central to return to St Budeaux on a Saturday evening in 1947, using the SR train that was worked by a GWR engine. The normal engine at that time was inevitably one of Laira's Moguls, but that evening he was amazed and overjoyed when 'VANCOUVER' ran in from Exmouth Junction shed to work the train. A GWR veteran worked a passenger train over the SR route via Okehampton! An exceptional treat but, unfortunately, at that period I was not recording dates in my notebooks.

The normal duties for Bulldogs during the 1930s and 1940s is depicted in this view of a down express climbing Dainton bank in 1937 hauled by a Castle class 4-6-0, piloted by un-named 'Bulldog' 3427 which was shedded at Laira. Both engines have steam to spare as they are 'blowing off' at their safety valves. The rear side of a speed restriction pointer is visible to the right of the train.

Newton Abbot was a good location to see Bulldogs, and here is that shed's 3430 'INCHCAPE' coupled to a 'Grange' class 4-6-0, waiting in the shed yard to take over a train to Plymouth on 26 May 1947. A 'Large Prairie' tank is partly hidden. This was another engine that was very familiar to our family, and I recall my mother telling me that the Inchcape was a rock on which a bell was positioned to warn unsuspecting shipping of its presence.

This was a very familiar scene at Laira shed to me during the period from 1945 to 1947. Un-named 'Bulldog' 3431 is in light steam, in the shed yard. Instead of the normal LA shed stencil, this engine had for a while LAIRA daubed along the underside of the frame. The front of a 4700 class 2-8-0 is visible next to the engine. Kenneth Brown

The deeper frames of Laira's 3441 'BLACKBIRD' are prominent in this almost side view of the engine taking a train of vans up through North Road during August 1948. Part of a 'small tank 45' can be seen at platform No.7. Ray Coxon

Another of Laira's faithful 'Bulldogs' was 3445 'FLAMINGO' which is standing in the shed's coal sidings in light steam on 21 August 1947. The author saw this engine on a summer Saturday afternoon in 1945 piloting a 'Castle' on a fourteen coach express, climbing St Austell bank. So much steam was issuing from the area around the inside cylinders between the frames that it engulfed the engine, and made reading the name and numberplate very difficult from the top of a cutting.   Kenneth Brown

Here, the third member of Laira's post war trio of 'Birds', 3446 'GOLDFINCH' is stabled on the same line circa 1946-47. The LA shed stencil is just discernible through the grime on the side of the frame.

Just before the Second World War Laira had a different pair of birds on its books. They were 3449 'NIGHTINGALE' and 3453 'SEAGULL', both old friends to the author. The first of these is piloting one of Laira's 'King' class 4-6-0s, 6016 'KING EDWARD V' on a down express which is climbing Tigley bank, between Totnes and Marley tunnel, during 1937. A.G.Ellis

One of Exeter shed's 'Bulldogs' 3451 'PELICAN' has emerged from the 205-yard long Kennaway tunnel and is approaching Dawlish on an up stopping passenger train on an unknown date, but probably pre 1940.

18

DUKE CLASS 4-4-0s

These beautifully designed locomotives were the mainstay of main line passenger services in Devon and Cornwall for many years prior to the Bulldogs becoming available in quantity. Even then they continued to have a presence in the area up to the late 1920s. They were designed to work trains over the steeply graded and sharply curved lines in the area, and for a while were called 'Devons', but in their early days they had been known as the 'Pendennis Castle' class. Strangely, this was the name of the second engine of the class that was built. As they were such a part of the everyday GWR scene in the area, I have included a goodly batch of photos to record these elegant locomotives. The author was lucky enough to see a few representatives of this class, but the nearest sighting to Devon was of 9083 'COMET' working an up train of vans between Taunton and Cogload. He saw it from a down train as it passed. The nameplate had been embellished to read *INCOMETAX* by adding stars and letters daubed on the nameplate in white.

With a gleaming brass dome and safety valve, 3259 'THE LIZARD' is at the head of an up train at Plymouth North Road in 1904 or 1905. The engine was re-numbered to 3258 and was named 'LIZARD' until January 1904. This was a long lived engine, which was built in September 1895 and lasted until February 1938.

Every part of 3274 'CORNISHMAN' shines as it stands in the yard at Millbay shed in 1905. This engine, which has lost it's brass dome, later became 3267. The elegantly designed outside frames and wheel springs are well depicted in this photo. The circular mark on the side of the engine's boiler is a 'blanking off' plate fitted where the boiler feed originally entered from the clack box. Clack boxes were removed from the locos.

This is a close up view of 3272 'FOWEY' at North Road in the 1920s. The driver talks to a rail-wayman, who is probably the train's guard, as he watches the coupling up procedure. This engine was originally numbered 3281 and was de-named in July 1930. A.G.Ellis

This is an interesting photo of 3275 'ST ERTH' on an up train of empty passenger stock between Devonport and Devonport Junction on an unknown but early date. The engine had started life as 3285 and lost its name in July 1930. The up line is formed of 'Bullhead' track whilst the Down line is still laid as 'Baulk Road'. A ganger relaxes as the train passes. Rail Archive Stephenson (Photomatic)

Here is 3275 'ST ERTH' again at the head of up empty passenger stock at North Road on 11 August 1923. A 'Saint' class 4-6-0 stands nearby.

This scene at North Road on 8 September 1921 has 3279 'TOR BAY' waiting to run to Laira sheds. It appears to have been detached from an up train but the tender still contains a good supply of coal. Originally this engine had been numbered 3290 and until December 1903 was named 'TORBAY'.

Having worked in on a down train, un-named 'Duke' 3282 waits at North Road on 9 August 1930 for the road to be set for it to back out to Laira sheds. Originally numbered 3314, this engine had been named 'CHEPSTOW CASTLE' until May 1923, when the name was required for newly constructed 'Castle' class 4-6-0 4077.

The old buildings, constructed of timber, show up well in this photo of 3284 'ISLE OF JERSEY' at North Road on an unknown date. It started life as 3317 and until January 1904 was named 'JERSEY'. To release the 32XX series of numbers for use on newly constructed 2251 class 0-6-0s, this engine was renumbered 9084 in October 1946.

Recorded at North Road during Whitsun 1901,this is 3319 'KATERFELTO' in original condition, with a straight nameplate mounted on the side of the boiler/firebox; it later became 3285. After 1903 the straight nameplate was replaced by one of curved pattern.

In this photo 3319 'KATERFELTO' has gained its curved nameplates, so the date is between early 1904 and 1912. It is on an up stopping passenger train at Bittaford Platform. Notice the standard GWR 'pagoda' shelter on each platform.

Rounding the curve north of Teignmouth on an up stopping passenger train is 3290 'SEVERN'. It was numbered 3328 before 1912. The fireman is hanging well out of the cab watching the photographer. Many years earlier the train would have been emerging from East Cliff tunnel at this point.

This side view study at North Road, taken pre 1904, shows 3329 'THAMES' at the head of a down train. It has a straight nameplate mounted on the side of a Belpaire firebox. This engine became 3291 and then in 1946 became 9091.

This is a pre 1904 photo at North Road of 3253 'PENDENNIS CASTLE'. Note that this engine has a straight nameplate that is mounted further forward on the side of the boiler. It is coupled to an up stopping passenger train. It changed its identity to become 3300, and was rebuilt to a 'Bulldog' class in November 1908.

An unidentified 'Duke' class locomotive worked the train for the opening ceremony of the branch line to Yealmpton, where the train has arrived on 15 January 1898. The engine has just broken the tape carrying suspended flags and banners and, because of the slow shutter speed used, the tape appears blurred. The lavishly decorated engine was specially re-named 'LADY MORLEY' for the day, as Lady Morley performed the opening ceremony. Unfortunately, historical records do not record the number of the locomotive involved. To know that one member of the class was re-named for one day, but to be unable to identify which member it was, to complete the locomotive history of the class, is frustrating.

19

OTHER GWR 4-4-0s

During the late 1890s and early 1900s Dean built several different classes of 4-4-0s that had larger driving wheels than were fitted to the Dukes and the Bulldogs. These classes handled all principal expresses east of Exeter, and on other routes from Paddington. Following on from the Bulldogs, there were four engines that were rebuilt from earlier 2-4-0s and constituted the No.7 or 'Armstrong 7 FT coupled' 4-4-0s. Next came the 'Badminton' class, some of which were later re-boilered and virtually became the forerunners of the later 'City' class. These were followed by the 'Atbaras' and the 'Flowers' which were Atbaras fitted with deeper frames. These were followed by the famous 'City' class which, until the arrival of the French 4-4-2s, handled most of the expresses between London, Bristol and Plymouth. Churchward followed on from Dean by constructing the inside framed 'County' class 4-4-0s. Lastly, in this section, a surprise was the rebuilding by the GWR of twenty nine members of the Bulldog class with Duke cabs and Duke type boilers between 1936 and 1939 to replace the ageing Duke class on trains in the Central Wales area. A few of this class were based in England and on rare occasions worked westward. These were officially called the 3200 or 'Earl' class but were nicknamed 'Dukedogs' by enthusiasts.

For a very brief period three of the 'Dukedogs' based in England were transferred to Newton Abbot for trials to assess their suitability as pilots over the South Devon banks. This must have been deemed unsatisfactory as they departed very shortly. Rounding the curve after ascending Hemerdon bank on 6 August 1955 with the 12.30 PM Newquay to Paddington is 'Castle class 4-6-0 5077 'FAIREY BATTLE' which is piloted by 'Dukedog' 9023 which was renumbered from 3223 in September 1946. Mike Daly

This shot taken after 1906 shows 'Badminton' class 3294 'BLENHEIM' in the yard at Millbay shed with the crew posing for the camera. This engine later became 4102.

Now we have 'Atbara' class 3408 'OPHIR' standing in the locomotive servicing yard at Kingswear, having been turned ready to work back to Newton Abbot. This was taken between October 1901 and September 1907. The engine was re-numbered to 3708 and in September 1907 it was re-named 'KILLARNEY' to work the first excursion to that resort from Paddington on 16th of that month. This was intended to be a temporary re-naming, but it became permanent.

The 'Armstrong 7 FT' 4-4-0s rarely worked west of Exeter, but on 3 August 1925 4172 Gooch is running into North Road tender first, coupled to another loco. Note the small nameplate affixed to the top of the splasher. A 'Half cab' pannier tank is shunting stock in the distance. This engine temporarily lost its name in 1900 when it was transferred to 2-2-2 No.1130.
Stephenson Locomotive Society

This is a very rare photo of 'Atbara' 3374 in Laira shed yard, named 'BRITANNIA' suitably decorated for working the Royal train. This engine was correctly called 'BADEN POWELL', but It was renamed 'PRETORIA' for one day only on 29 October 1900 to work a special train. It was renamed 'BRITANNIA' for Royal train duties on 7 March and 10 March 1902 so it is at Laira on one of those dates. Then it was renamed 'KITCHENER' to work another special train on 12 July 1902. It later became 4121.

Here is 'Abtara' 4127 'LADYSMITH' heading an up express along the sea wall between Teignmouth and Parson's tunnel on an undated murky, damp, day. It had previously been numbered 3380. The fireman is watching the photographer.

'Flower' class 4161 (previously 4113) 'HYACINTH' has just coupled to an up express at North Road on 22 August 1925. The deepness of the frames is apparent. The fireman is attending to the tools and coal on the tender. Until May 1916 the name had been 'HYACINTHE'. Stephenson Locomotive Society

Almost brand new, in immaculate condition at the throat of Laira shed yard, is 'City' class 3433 'CITY OF BATH' early in 1903; it later became 3710. On 14 July 1903 this engine, under the control of Driver Burden, was in charge of the down 'Cornishman' which was the 10.40am Paddington to Penzance. The train was conveying the Prince of Wales to Plymouth on that date for a Royal visit. With a Locomotive Inspector on the footplate and permission to 'disregard the timetable' they departed and soon reached 75mph. They attained 87mph descending Dauntsey bank and again when in Box tunnel. The train covered the 245¾ miles to North Road in 233½ minutes. This gave an arrival at North Road that was thirty seven minutes ahead of the schedule, following an extremely lively performance by this loco. This could well be the day when this photo was taken after the engine had run to Laira shed for servicing.

No collection of photos of this area would be complete unless one is included of record breaking 3440 (ex 3717) 'CITY OF TRURO', which is passing Britannia Halt as it approaches Kingswear on 19 May 1957. The engine had worked a special train to Kingswear and had returned to Newton Abbot shed for servicing, but it was not turned there. So it returned from Newton Abbot to be turned at Kingswear with a Locomotive Inspector on the footplate. This engine is reputed to have attained 102.3 MPH on 9 May 1904, in the hands of driver Moses Clements, during the descent of Wellington bank whilst working an Ocean Mails special from Plymouth. The Inspector had told Clements that Churchward had said "They could go and break their bloody necks" to beat the times that the LSWR were making on the run from Plymouth to London. Maurice Dart

We end this section with 'County class 4-4-0 3478 'COUNTY OF DEVON' on the end of the coaling line at Laira shed on an unknown date. However, as the engine carries one of the experimental liveries with plain sans-serif letters, on the tender we know that it was taken between 1904 and 1906. F. Pascoe.

SOUTHERN 4-4-0s

The LSWR used various types of 4-4-0s in Devon to work passenger and goods trains for many years. Indeed the faithful T9s, nicknamed 'Greyhounds, were still operating in the area for several years after the arrival of 'West Country' class Pacifics. The other 4-4-0 types ceased to visit Plymouth in the late 1940s.

The crew pose on T9 class 280 outside the rarely photographed shed yard at Devonport LSWR. The engine is in original condition and this side view shows the graceful lines of these lively fast locomotives. As the engine shed closed in 1908 this scene must pre-date that year. This engine, together with 289, was still working from Friary shed in the mid-1940s. They had superceded the earlier C8 class 4-4-0s.

A pair of T9s, 717 and 713, carrying different liveries, double–head an up express that has departed from Plymouth Friary and is passing the later Friary engine shed, probably in the 1930s.

During a visit to Friary shed one enthusiast poses for another on K10 class 340, probably in the early 1920s. These engines were known as 'Small Hoppers'.

An enlarged version of the K10 was developed. Known as the L11 class or 'Large Hoppers', they were more powerful and faster. One of them, standing in the sun at Friary shed in 1923, is 436.

Another photo taken at Devonport LSWR before 1908 shows S11 class 4-4-0 399 outside the shed. This class had greater diameter driving wheels, larger cylinders and a larger boiler than the L11s. Several young and older admirers gaze at the engine from the wall above.

We end this section with earlier smaller X6 class 4-4-0 666 in the yard outside Friary shed, probably in the 1920s.

FOUR COUPLED TANK ENGINES

This section commences with one of the few GWR 4-4-0 tank locomotives. This was unusual for the GWR in being a one-off type and it worked for quite a number of years in Cornwall and Devon. Next come the several classes of 0-4-4 tanks that were used in the Plymouth area. They are followed by branch line tank locomotives of the 2-4-0 and 0-4-2 wheel arrangement. The section ends with small 0-4-0 tanks that were used by the GWR and the LSWR for shunting work at the docks and yards around Plymouth.

This is the lone example of a GWR 4-4-0 ST type. It was rebuilt from a 2-4-2T. The photo was taken during 1906 and shows No.13 on an unusually long train departing from Churston for Brixham. The open wagon in the consist may have been used to accommodate passengers' luggage, which at that period usually consisted of bulky portmanteaus and other large items. Notice that the branch platform has its own waiting shelter and the door of the adjacent 'Railway Hotel is open to receive guests. This engine later spent many years working on the line to Looe, followed by a period at Plymouth before it ended its days at Swindon. Rail Archive Stephenson(Photomatic)

This historic photo shows one of the GWR's 3521 class 0-4-4Ts departing from Plymouth Millbay. The engines of this class were built as broad gauge 0-4-2 STs in 1888-89 and were converted to 0-4-4Ts in 1890-91. They were altered to standard gauge in 1891-92 and were further converted to 4-4-0 tender engines between 1899 and 1902. It is hauling the first standard gauge train to leave from the station on 23 May 1892. This was the Monday following the weekend when the entire remaining broad gauge track on the GWR had been converted to standard gauge. An 0-6-0 ST is on passenger stock on the left, whilst to the right, another loco, possibly a 517 class 0-4-2T, is on a train in the goods section of the station. A wooden sleeper blocks uncompleted trackwork on one of the nearby lines. The goods shed is seen on the right and the 'Duke of Cornwall Hotel' rises above the station on the left. The line to Millbay docks descends an incline between the goods station and the goods shed. This line passed over a level crossing and the adjacent pedestrian footbridge is visible in the background.

Large LSWR M7 class 0-4-4T 252 is alongside Friary shed, raised up under the hoist with its rear bogie removed for attention, probably in the 1930s. These locos worked suburban trains from Friary to Tavistock and Brentor until the late 1950s.   A.G.Ellis

Smaller and lighter than M7s were LSWR O2 class 0-4-4Ts. These were used from Friary to work the services on the line to Turnchapel and also on the branch line from Bere Alston to Callington. In the early 1920s 211 is near Oreston with a train to Turnchapel.   H.Gordon Tidey

The driver on LSWR T1 class 0-4-4T 12 peeps from the cab as the engine stands on the centre road at Plymouth Friary, probably in the 1920s. It had just removed the stock of the train that had arrived with the engine which is backing out on the left. The mark crossing the lower right part of the photo is caused by a crack in the photographic plate. T1s worked trains to Tavistock until the late 1940s and the author saw 3 and 7 quite regularly, but this loco was withdrawn during January 1933.

The driver on T1 14 waits to depart from North Road and watches for the signal arm to drop. It is working a train from Tavistock to Friary in the early 1920s. This engine was withdrawn in July 1933.

One of the first batch of famous GWR 'Metro' 2-4-0Ts in the yard at Newton Abbot shed during 1932 is 470. This class gained their name as many of them worked trains over the 'Widened lines' from Paddington in their early years. At first they had open cabs, and were fitted with condensing gear for this work. They came in three sizes, small, medium and large! Many were long-lived and were to be found over most of the GWR system. This loco entered service in April 1869 and was withdrawn from Newton Abbot in February 1934.

One of the third batch of GWR 'Metro' tanks built in January 1899 was 3581 which is at Newton Abbot on an 'Auto' train. This engine was allocated here for several periods between 1934 and 1940. The author was lucky to see this engine on several occasions in 1944 when passing through Lostwithiel, where it was waiting with the 'Auto' train to Fowey. It was withdrawn from St Blazey shed in November 1945. Notice the NA stencil on the side of the lamp on the front of the engine. According to an inscription on the reverse of this photo, the right hand tank fitted to the engine was repaired during April 1936. Compare the riveting on the tank with that on the tank fitted to 470 in the previous photo.

The crew pose on a very clean unidentified 'Metro' tank as it waits at Avonwick in the early 1900s with a train for Kingsbridge.

The final light branch 'Auto-fitted' passenger engines on the GWR were the 4800 class 0-4-2Ts. Newton Abbot and Exeter each had a sizeable allocation whilst Laira had to wait until the BR period to gain any members of the type. One of Laira's engines, 1434, is arriving at Yelverton in the late 1950s with an 'Auto' train from Tavistock South to Plymouth. A haze of smoky exhaust almost obscures the mouth of the tunnel in the background. At the end of 1946 the 4800s were renumbered to the 14XX series to release their original numbers for use by 2800 and 2884 class 2-8-0s which were being converted to oil-firing.   Mike Daly

The Ashburton 'Auto' train is in the up platform at Totnes with trailer 132 hauled by 4865 in June 1936. This loco went to Newton Abbot and to Ashburton sub-shed when built new in February of that year.   W.Potter

Prior to the arrival of the 4800 class, members of the much older 517 class 0-4-2Ts worked services on the Ashburton branch. An 'Auto' train composed of trailer 130, hauled by 1163, has arrived at the down platform at Totnes, probably in the 1920s.

Two strangers, which originated on the London, Brighton and South Coast Railway, came to Plymouth for a period. They were D1 class 0-4-2Ts, one of which, B358, waits at Friary to depart for Turnchapel. This would have been in the period between 1930 and 1932. The other D1 was B259. B signified an SR Central division engine under the responsibility of Brighton Works. Similarly A denoted Ashford for Eastern division locos whilst E was for Western division locos maintained at Eastleigh. These D1s worked some branch line trains in the South West prior to members of the O2 class being fitted with 'Auto' gear. Stephenson Locomotive Society

This is a rare photo of GWR 0-4-0 ST 1329 shunting at Millbay docks in the early 1900s. It was originally a South Devon Railway broad gauge loco numbered 2175 and named 'RAVEN'. Modified to standard gauge and numbered 1329 it was withdrawn in March 1910 and was almost immediately sold to the Wantage Tramway. It was finally cut up by that railway during 1920.

Standing in the shed yard at Newton Abbot in the 1920s is 517 class 1439 which had retained it's 'Half-cab'. This engine was withdrawn in September 1930.

The LSWR B4 class 0-4-0 Ts were part of the railway scene around Plymouth Friary since the first members of the class, 85,86 and 87 were sent there, brand new, in 1891. Various, but not all, members of the class of twenty five locos have worked from Friary over the years. Some were for very brief periods, for example when one of the shed's own engines was away for repair. Three examples of this were when 176 'GUERNSEY' was present in August 1945, followed by 81 'JERSEY' in 1945 or 1946. Most unexpectedly 30082 came down from May to July 1957. The named examples came from Southampton Docks shed, whilst 30082 was from Eastleigh. Standing in the yard at Friary shed on 8 September 1924 are 100 and 91, both still lettered LSWR, with O2 class 0-4-4T 177 at the rear. Stephenson Locomotive Society

As stated in the previous caption, named examples of the B4s appeared a couple of times at Friary shed, on loan from Southampton Docks shed where all of the named examples were based. However as some of Friary's residents were either withdrawn or transferred away in the late 1940s, to our surprise three of the named examples were transferred down to replace them. They did not retain their names very long after arriving. They were 95 'HONFLEUR', 89 'TROUVILLE' and 102 'GRANVILLE'. When they arrived they only carried their name on the side of the tank, with their number on the front and rear buffer beams. Alongside Friary shed, soon after arrival in 1946, is 95 Honfleur with O2 class 0-4-4T 192 to the right, up on blocks with its rear bogie removed. Stephenson Locomotive Society.

GWR OIL-BURNERS, GAS TURBINES, BROAD GAUGE, SINGLE WHEELERS AND STEAM RAIL MOTORS

This section covers several batches of locomotives, which comprise groups that are too small to warrant separation. The first is a selection of GWR locomotives that were converted to burn oil during the fuel crisis of 1947 and ran in that condition for up to a couple of years before reverting to coal burning. These are followed by shots of the two experimental gas turbine locomotives that operated on the Western Region of British Railways in the early 1950s. Next is a batch of photos of GWR broad gauge locomotives that only ran until 1892. The section ends with a couple of shots of steam rail motors. These were either scrapped or converted to trailer cars for use in Auto trains.

In 1947 a pair of GWR oil-burners stand alongside the fuelling point that was established by the side of the New shed. The front engine is 2800 class 2-8-0 4808(ex 2834) and at the rear is 'Hall' class 4-6-0 3955(ex 6949) 'HABERFIELD HALL'. As they did not burn coal these oil-burners were usually spotlessly clean externally. The oil tanks are visible in the locomotives tenders. Notice the shutters on the side of cab. These were a wartime measure to cut out glare from the fire. Kenneth Brown

In the extensive yard behind the coaler at Laira shed in 1947 is oil-burning 'Castle' class 4-6-0 5079 'LYSANDER'. Whereas the oil-burning 'Halls' and 2-8-0s were renumbered, the 'Castles' and the solitary Mogul that were converted retained their original numbers. I recall seeing this engine soon after it arrived back at Laira following conversion. It was stabled inside the round-house just around to the right from the entrance and we were able to walk around it to examine it and admire the gleaming paintwork and brass. The shutters remain by the cab windows.

The GWR ordered two experimental gas turbine locomotives, but both of them were delivered after the formation of British Railways. The first was known as the 'Brown-Boveri' loco and was numbered 18000. It is entering North Road on 22 February 1950 early in the afternoon on completion of its first trial run from Paddington. Notice the complete absence of observers in the famous 'lane' that overlooks the station. It was withdrawn in 1960, and after a period in store it returned to its home in Switzerland where it was used in experiments. It returned to this country early in 1994 and is an exhibit at The Railway Age at Crewe. Maurice Dart

The second gas turbine was numbered 18100 and was known as the 'Metro-Vick' locomotive. It is entering North Road at the end of its first trial run from Paddington on 4 March 1952. On this occasion there are quite a number of observers by the overline bridge and in the 'lane'. This loco-motive was out of use by the end of 1953 but was not withdrawn until early in 1958. It was rebuilt into a straight Electric loco and numbered E1001, and was to be used for both training purposes and testing overhead line equipment. Near the end of 1959 it was again renumbered, becoming E2001. In this guise it worked at various locations in connection with electrification schemes. After a period in store inside Rugby testing station it was withdrawn in April 1968. After several moves it was sold for scrap in September 1972, being cut up around January 1973.   Maurice Dart

These are three views of the first broad gauge locomotive in this collection. The engine started life as South Devon Railway 2172 and was named 'OWL'. In November 1890 it was sold to Pearson & Son, contractors, and was then bought back from them by the GWR in June 1893. The GWR converted it to standard gauge and renumbered it 1327; it survived until scrapped in April 1913. These views were taken at a quarry loading point at Cornwood whilst it was working for Pearson on widening work.   A. G. Ellis collection

This is classic view of GWR, ex South Devon Railway, broad gauge 2-4-0 ST 2137 'PRINCE' at Brixham in 1890. It was built in June 1871 and was converted to standard gauge June 1893 and became 1316. It was withdrawn in May 1899 but its history after that is extremely interesting. In March 1896 it was converted to a winding engine and worked at Crofton from May of that year until April 1897. Then next, from March 1898, it was used at Stert as a pumping engine until May 1899 when it was condemned. However, it was then despatched to Portreath for use as a stationary winding engine and numbered 0301, but it was not withdrawn from stock until 1901. In June 1904 it moved to Swindon and then to Old Oak Common in November 1905. It moved again as a 'spare' to Swindon machinery stores in August 1906 and amazingly, in November 1917 it was sent to work at a Prisoner of War camp at Dorchester, from where it was returned to Swindon again two years later, again being held as 'spare'. From November 1923 it was used as a portable boiler but was once again in store as 'spare' by May 1928. This lasted until September 1933 when it was again classed as 'spare'. Finally after spending much time on the dump it was cut up in August 1935.

This is ex Bristol & Exeter Railway broad gauge 4-4-0 ST 86 at Torquay. This engine, which was built by the Avonside Engine Company in December 1872, became GWR 2049 and was withdrawn during May 1892.

A scene at Ivybridge before May 1892 has ex South Devon Railway broad gauge 4-4-0 ST 'LANCE' on a train for Plymouth. The engine was built by the Avonside Engine Company during February 1875 and became GWR 2130. It was withdrawn from service in May 1892, but saw use at Swindon works for shunting broad gauge stock until June 1893. The builder's plate is in a prominent position below the lamp on the back of the bunker. A broad gauge tender loco is 'waiting for the road' on the up line. Notice that the ballast has been scraped back ready for the wooden transoms to be cut, indicating that this photo was taken very shortly before the broad gauge was abolished.   R.Handsford-Worth

Two 'Single Wheelers' are at Newton Abbot on a date between 1895 and 1911. Nearer to the camera with the crew posing, is 3049 'NELSON' and in the background at the shed yard throat is 3018 'RACER', which was renamed 'GLENSIDE' during September 1911. This engine was built in April 1892 as a 2-2-2, but was converted to a 3031 'Achilles' class 4-2-2 during August 1894. This class was originally built for working West of England expresses between Paddington and Newton Abbot. The diameter of the driving wheel was 7ft 8½ in.

Between 1903 and 1908 the GWR built a series of steam rail motor cars. These were carriages which contained a steam locomotive boiler and a driving compartment in one end. They were used on local suburban services but were underpowered and withdrawn, with some being converted to 'Auto Trailers'. A train from Saltash to Plymouth Millbay is stopped at Ford Halt on an unknown date. It is composed of two steam railmotors with a small carriage in between them. This small station was closed in 1941 after receiving extensive damage during one of the Blitz raids.

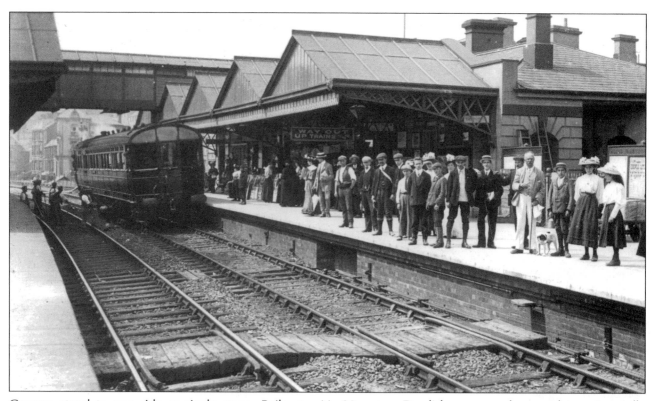

Gangers stand to one side as single steam Railmotor No.33 enters Dawlish on an unknown date. A goodly compliment of passengers are more interested in the photographer than in the approaching train as they wait on the platform, whilst others inspect what is on offer at the bookstall. This steam railmotor ceased working during December 1922.

23

DIESEL LOCOMOTIVES

This section of the collection brings the story of locomotives in the area from 1958 up to date. The first diesels in the area were, surpringly, four small diesel mechanical shunters which arrived at Friary shed late in April 1957. Some 350 HP diesel electric shunters that came to Laira in May 1958 followed them. Meanwhile early main line diesel hydraulics came to Laira from May 1958. Photographs of these diesels at that time are very hard to find. The majority of enthusiasts, myself included, simply recorded their numbers as they were replacing our beloved steam locos. We really did not want to acknowledge their presence apart from recording their numbers, let alone photographing them. Various classes of Western Region diesel hydraulics followed, to be gradually replaced by diesel electric locos. Suddenly we realised that the early diesels, which we had rarely photographed, were no longer with us, as they were replaced by more modern diesel electric locos. A classic example of this was the short lived diesel servicing depot at Belmont, outside Millbay station, virtually on the site of Millbay steam shed. I looked across the tracks several times from the entrance gate of Millbay carriage shed to view the early diesel locos that were present, but no way would I (at the time) waste film photographing them! In hindsight we had 'tunnel vision'!

The first diesel mechanical shunters that arrived at Friary were four class O4s. Laira later received a couple of class O3s and then the O4s at Friary were replaced by some other O3s. One of this third batch of 204 HP diesel mechanical shunters was D2177 which is shunting wagons at Victoria wharves at the extreme end of the Cattewater branch line sometime in 1966.

A batch of 350 HP diesel electric shunters numbered from D3509 to D3527 came to Laira and then moved around the area. They were replaced by newer members of the class, one of which, D4010 is on station pilot duty at Plymouth in the 1960s. This engine became 08442.

A modern scene has EWS owned, diesel electric shunter, 08405 moving loaded CDA wagons around the Imerys Minerals works at Marsh Mills on 29 October 2005. It is slowly moving wagons over a weighbridge in order to record the weight of clay that has been loaded.   Maurice Dart

The class 09 was a 400 HP variation of class 08 with slightly increased speed. Initially they were all based on the Southern Region, but after many years the class dispersed over a wide area. On 24 November 2004, wagons that have been loaded with metal scrap near Laira wharf are being propelled up the gradient, past the site of Cattewater Junction, to Friary by 09013. A reversal would take place at Friary to enable the train to run to Tavistock Junction yard via Laira. Maurice Dart

The first main line diesels in the area were the five North British built 'Warship' class hydraulics of which D603 'CONQUEST' is on an up passenger passing North Road West to enter Plymouth during 1962.

The D600s were soon followed by the D800 'Warship' class hydraulics that consisted of seventy one locos. At Plymouth in the 1960s D838 'RAPID' is in platform 5. The up 'Royal Duchy' is in platform 7 in charge of D867 'ZENITH'.

Next to arrive on the scene were the largely unsuccessful smaller North British Class 22 diesel hydraulics. During 1969, D6307 is passing through Plymouth with an up goods one morning at 10.35 AM.

The next class that was seen was the class 35 'Hymeks'. Members of the type that were based at Cardiff Canton started appearing on trains from that city, after which Laira and Newton Abbot were each allocated a few. They penetrated into Cornwall infrequently, but were also used on trains on the ex SR route via Okehampton. On 13 August 1964, Newton Abbot based D7068 is passing Mutley with the empty stock of a train from Exeter Central via Okehampton to Plymouth. It is bound for Friary which had closed to passengers on 15 September 1958. Maurice Dart

The final form of hydraulics to appear were the well designed class 52 'Westerns', of which D1057 'WESTERN CHIEFTAIN' is passing Laira shed with an up express during April 1974.

Diesel electrics started appearing and the intermediate sized class 25s became a familiar sight in the area. A pair of these, 25159 and 25101 pass Langstone Cliff, near Dawlish Warren with a down express on 16 July 1977. Some camping coaches are in the upside sidings in the distance.

Increasing in size we see Class 37 diesel electric 37676 stabled in Park sidings at Plymouth on 9 November 2003. These locos worked china clay traffic in the area.   Maurice Dart

'Peak' class diesel electric locos appeared on trains to and from the Midlands and the North of England. Class 45 45076 is on a down passenger at Dawlish, probably in the 1980s.

The class 46s were similar to the class 45s but were fitted with different traction motors and generators. Standing in the carriage sidings at Goodrington, next to a diesel multiple unit, in the 1980s is 46020.

The largest class of diesel electrics built was the class 47s. They were used on a variety of traffic including, more recently, Mail trains. In Park sidings at Plymouth with Royal Mail stock on 4 August 1998 are 47788 'CAPTAIN PETER MANISTY RN' and 47780. Maurice Dart

Following the retirement of the 'non-standard' 'Westerns', main line passenger trains in the area were handled by class 47s and also the entire fleet of diesel electric class 50s, which had themselves been displaced by the electrification of the West Coast main line. 50031 'HOOD' passes platform 8 at Newton Abbot with the 11.20am Penzance to Paddington as single car DMU 55025 sits in the erstwhile platform 9 on 30 July 1980.

A common sight now are the powerful class 66 locos that are normally seen on freight trains. However, several special excursions were run to Devon and Cornwall for the total eclipse of the sun on 11 August 1999, and most were hauled by class 66 locos. One of those waiting to depart from Plymouth is 66037, in charge of the return Pathfinder Tour to Crewe, that left at 18.10. Maurice Dart

On 1 November 2005 a rake of HST stock left Heaton depot, Newcastle bound for Laira. It recessed overnight at Willesden. It is passing Totnes on a wet 2 November hauled by GB Rail Freight 66717 with a 'BLUEBIRDS ON TOUR' headboard with 73204 and 73205 acting as Barrier vehicles.   Maurice Dart

Apart from variations of class 66, the other new type to appear was class 67, members of which monopolised the working of mail trains. Two members of the class, 67007 and 67022 wait at the Post Office terminal at Plymouth on mail stock late morning on a very wet and cold 23 December 2003.   Maurice Dart

24

INDUSTRIAL LOCOMOTIVES

Some industrial concerns possessed their own railway and locomotives, but very few photos of these are available for this area of Devon. Several present day establishments possess diesel locos, most of which are inaccessible to the public. A small selection of views of some of these from the past completes this book.

The Royal Naval Dockyard at Devonport has had its own internal railway system since 1867, and a selection of locomotives has operated over it and continues to do so on the much truncated layout. In the North yard in the 1950s is 0-4-0 ST No.13 that was built by Andrew Barclay in 1915 and carried their Works No.1397. It was scrapped sometime after January 1959.   Mike Daly

Victoria wharves at Plymouth have enjoyed various owners, who have possessed locomotives. Powell & Hugh were succeeded by Coast Lines and their 0-4-0 ST *Alicie* is on the wharves in the 1920s or 1930s. This engine, which had originally been an 0-6-0 ST, was built by Hunslet Engine Co. (No.366) in 1886. It had originally worked at Bristol but had arrived at Pymouth by at least November 1917 and was sold for scrap in 1935. Stephenson Locomotive Society

The four foot six inch gauge Lee Moor Tramway, which ran north east from Plymouth, possessed a pair of 0-4-0 STs that were built by Peckett in 1899. They worked between the top of Cann Wood self-acting incline and the china clay and brick works at Torycombe, just below the village of Lee Moor. In about 1921 'LEE MOOR NO.2' has stopped on the level crossing at Torycombe with a train of loaded wagons bound for Laira Wharf. China clay kilns form a backdrop. This loco was works No.784 and may be seen at Buckfastleigh where it is in a separate shed on a short length of track. English China Clays

We end this varied selection of locomotive views with 3ft gauge 0-4-2T 'C. A. HANSON' on the Redlake Railway. It is on a train of empty wagons near the top of the incline which climbed up from Cantrell works where there was a GWR siding. The engine, which was Works No.1228 built by Kerr Stuart in 1911, was scrapped in 1921. The clay works, which was north of Ivybridge, closed in 1932 and the line was dismantled during 1933.

Goodbye Gay Meadow

THE HOME OF SHREWSBURY TOWN FOOTBALL CLUB 1910-2007

GOODBYE GAY MEADOW
First edition published in 2007 by Matthew Ashton
in association with Shrewsbury Town Football Club

Text and Design © Matthew Ashton 2007

Art Direction: Jim Lockwood

For all queries concerning this publication please write to:
Matthew Ashton
PO Box 979
Shrewsbury
SY3 7XB
UK
info@matthewashton.com
www.matthewashton.com

Printed in Singapore 2007

21 40 19 05 20 07 01

A CIP catalogue for this book is available from the British Library

ISBN 978-0-9556518-0-9

Goodbye Gay Meadow

THE HOME OF SHREWSBURY TOWN FOOTBALL CLUB 1910-2007

Matthew Ashton

Published in association with Shrewsbury Town FC

As a football fan from Germany I am very fascinated by football stadiums. I love British grounds, because they are more traditional than those in my home country. They are full of character and the sites are not somewhere in the outskirts but near the centre of their towns. Some years ago I discovered a book called 'The Football Grounds of Great Britain' written by Simon Inglis. I avidly read chapter by chapter about history and ground description of every single British league ground. The most interesting story was not the one about Anfield, nor Hillsborough or even the other famous venues. The ground description about Gay Meadow attracted most of my interest. Inglis describes the Riverside as "One of the most charming sides of any football ground." He tells us that "Gay Meadow's appeal lies in its location" and that "all around are definite sights, that could only belong to Shrewsbury." He continues, that "Gay Meadow not only reflects the town of Shrewsbury but is a inescapable part of it."

I had never heard about Shrewsbury, so I looked it up on the map. A German tourist guide told me some facts about a charming mediaeval town in Shropshire. The fascination about Shrewsbury, the football club and especially Gay Meadow grew. So did my dream of visiting Gay Meadow on a match day. I wanted to catch the spirit of this unique venue. When I heard about the relocation to the New Meadow in 2007, I quickly decided to let the dream come true. I took a plane to Birmingham and arrived at Shrewsbury by train in the afternoon of October 7th 2006. That evening the Shrews would play against Macclesfield Town.

After having left my luggage in the hotel I crossed the bridge over the River Severn to the beloved ground to take some photographs. The staff were so kind to let me in. I strolled along the terraces, took the photographs and had some good talks with the groundsmen, who were preparing the pitch for the match. It was a very peaceful atmosphere four hours before kick-off. Afterwards, I had enough time to visit the lovely town, not missing a stop at a pub. When I set off for the match it began to drizzle. The floodlights were glowing. At half past seven I entered through the turnstile to the Riverside. I found a place in the middle of the terrace and enjoyed it, simply standing on "One of the most charming sides of any football ground," among all the Shropshire lads and cheering on Town (who won 2-1). After my first visit I booked a flight to watch the last match against Grimsby Town.

Hans-Peter Hauck – Aschaffenburg, Germany

And so dear friends, my time has passed - it's time for me to go,
this football game could be my last, the river told me so.
I almost made my century, and tears may flow from some,
although I knew eventually - the end would have to come.
But many things my eyes have seen and let me tell you how,
some of the things that there have been, from nineteen ten 'til now.

Cuzz – Whitchurch

My first game at Gay Meadow was October 13th 1962. My mum was a keen fan, having supported Shrewsbury since going with her father in 1930. On this wonderful autumnal day we walked down the street knocking on the doors of my friends and gradually collected a number of us. It was a great feeling to go down the Narrows with lots of other fans. We stood by the wall to the right of the goal and took in the vista that was spread before us, this resplendent green turf. We could smell the tobacco from the pipes that were being smoked in those days.

Ron Morgan – Shrewsbury

It was a sunny day as I set out to see my first Shrewsbury Town game. As I walked from the bus station along the river, I could smell the blossom on the trees. It was the 1992-93 season and the match was against Bury. I went along with a mate of mine from school, we got into the ground and stood on the Wakeman End. My one memory was seeing a very traditional ground with lots of energy around it and the old scoreboard in the corner. After that game I was hooked and have been an avid supporter ever since.

Andy Saunders – Bayston Hill, Shrewsbury

I had for the previous seasons taken my son down to the Meadow and he had witnessed our slow decline down the leagues. My admiration for his loyalty was immense and when we drew Everton in the FA Cup, I retold stories of previous higher league clubs that had come unstuck at the Meadow.

However, a cruel twist was to enter the scenario when my mother-in-law died suddenly on Boxing Day, the week before the game. When the funeral was arranged for the Saturday of the Everton game at noon at an isolated church in South Shropshire, it looked as though we would not make the game.

My wife insisted we went, "It is what mum would want you to do" she said, so my son and I attended the funeral and then drove up to Shrewsbury. We stopped in a lay-by near Cressage to change from dark suits into blue and amber. The rest is history.

When the curtain comes down it will be a very sad day as Gay Meadow has become my second home.

Andrew Muir – Harmer Hill

My first match was against Mansfield Town on November 1st 1997. My dad decided to take me and my brother to the Town match after failing to get tickets for Wolves v Middlesbrough. When he asked if we fancied going to watch Shrewsbury Town, we replied "Who?"

We parked at the Abbey car park and seeing the Gay Meadow floodlights in the distance got me very excited. We walked down the Narrows and bought a ticket for the Centre Stand.

I will always remember the atmosphere in the ground when we scored. Town won 3-2 on a very decent pitch and ever since that day in November I have been a huge Shrewsbury Town fan, and a season ticket holder for six years. Secretly I was a Manchester United supporter before watching the Town. I have now turned my back on them and support the Town through thick and thin.

Thanks for the memories Gay Meadow.

Sean Evans – Shrewsbury

It's not the FA Cup games and the promotion parties that I will remember, it's the autumnal days when the leaves fell from the back of the Riverside onto the pitch creating a lovely spectacle. I like to think that I have seen the best of the Meadow (in her twilight years), the old ground in Shrewsbury that was content with itself and didn't care what anyone else thought.

Glyn Price – Shrewsbury

The decrepit nature of the stadium simply added to the unique character, along with the sight of the crisp, brown autumn leaves drifting on the pitch.

Daniel Purchase – Whitchurch

The story behind the Weetabix appearing whenever Bristol Rovers play Shrewsbury started a few seasons ago before a league match at Gay Meadow. A few Gasheads got together and raised some money for the trip up to Shrewsbury. They hired a coach for the day after which about £300 was left in the kitty.

So it was decided to go to the pub before the game where £200 was stuck behind the bar to pay for drinks. After a while, a few Gasheads started feeling hungry but unfortunately the pub didn't serve food. The landlord then told them there was a supermarket nearby for them to get food and that he wouldn't mind them eating it in the pub.

A lonesome Gashead was then dispatched to fetch the grub with £75 after taking out the £25 owed to the coach driver. At the time this Gashead was slightly the worse for drink and returned to the pub armed with £75 worth of Weetabix. They took all of their stuff into the ground, and noticed some birds on the pitch. Being the kind souls that they are, they decided to feed them all of their Weetabix. By the time they had finished throwing them liberally around the terraces, the penalty area in front of the away section had turned from green to brown.

A few years later Rovers played Shrewsbury again and the same group were seen wearing T-shirts with 'Weetabix Invasion of Gay Meadow' on them and of course throwing plenty of Weetabix around. Unfortunately whenever Rovers now play Shrewsbury, the police are instructed to confiscate all forms of breakfast cereal at the game.

Peter Stump – Berkeley, Gloucestershire

The Gay Meadow will always hold good and bad memories. From ecstasy to the depths of despair, but they are memories that will be carried to the grave.

Colin James – Wistanstow

It can be easy to grow attached to things, and in an age where so many new football grounds are created with so little to separate them from each other, a ground as individual as the Meadow becomes even more precious. I feel so fortunate to have been able to spend so many happy (or even unhappy) times in a place that I always found special and unique in its appeal.

Paul Gladwell – Edinburgh

Pointing to a V-formation of birds flying over the Meadow during the Everton match in 2003, with about twenty minutes left and saying to my mates, "Look, it is a sign. We are going to win."

David Brown – London

It was my first wife's brother who got married on the day that the Town were playing in that infamous cup game against Manchester City. The reception was at the Railway Club. At 2.30 I dropped the bombshell that I was off to the match. To everyone's amazement the groom announced that he was coming as well. Later, needless to say, I got the blame for leading him on. I hasten to add that was not the reason she was my first wife – that is another story all together.

Rod Turner – Shrewsbury

One last pint in the Seven Stars and then at 7.25pm then we used to run like mad on the roads to get into the ground before kick-off. That was the luxury of being a Shrewsbury Town fan, even though we want to be in Division One and be successful with big crowds, the location of the ground meant lots of socialising in the pub and a guarantee of seeing kick-off.

Peter King – Shrewsbury

Living in Abbey Foregate, walking down past the Abbey and under the railway bridge, you could always tell if it was going to be a big crowd by looking at the amount of people coming over the English Bridge from Wyle Cop. In the 1950s when people did not own cars like they do today, the pavements were full and fans would walk about four abreast on the roadside.

Mike Jones – Shrewsbury

I will miss walking to the ground through town. It gets the vibe going before you actually get there.
Darren De Banks – St Albans

My love affair with Gay Meadow kicked off on December 10th 1970 against Preston North End watched by over 8,000 spectators. My father built the game up by pointing out that we were taking on a team that had won the League and Cup double, however he didn't say when this feat was achieved!

Watching a game under floodlights is so much more atmospheric. When Preston ran onto the Gay Meadow pitch in their bright white shirts and dark shorts, it looked like we were playing England. Because of the size of the crowd I was bundled on top of one of the concrete blocks by the old scoreboard, underneath the floodlights.

As a ten year old it was a wondrous sight to behold as the floodlights lit up the ground. Having only previously seen a football match on a black and white television, the colours, smells and noise of the crowd were unforgettable. Whilst we lost the match, I had caught the bug that would stay with me for the next 35 years.

That evening I skipped all the way home alongside my father talking of nothing other than the match I had just witnessed. For the next three years I did not miss a home game.

At the age of 13 my parents decided to relocate to Southport. It was a sad time as it also witnessed Shrewsbury's relegation to the bottom division in 1974. Despite a few visits to Haig Avenue to watch Southport, I realised Shrewsbury was still my first love.

At the age of 17 and with a driving licence in hand, I was back at the Meadow to witness the dawn of the Graham Turner era and the magical years we enjoyed in the Second Division.

Hugh Dennis – Holmeswood, Lancashire

I feel very lucky that I went to the Wakeman School. We used to be able to look out from our form room on the third floor and have a great view of the players training. I used to hand my autograph book in to the club when the big teams came down to get all the famous names to sign it.

David Morgan – Stoke-on-Trent

My passion started about thirty years ago when I attended the Wakeman School. Dinner breaks were spent down the sides and the back of the Meadow copping a fag with regular sightings of the players. On a goalpost painted on the back of the Station End I went in goal for Ian Atkins.

Bob Martin – Shrewsbury

I used to go to the Wakeman School and when it was a night match, I used to try to avoid the caretakers and open the big narrow windows overlooking the ground to watch the match. Of course, being mad keen I used to try to get autographs and as a young lad during lunch break, I used to watch the players train on that awful cinder pitch on the back of the Station End, which is now a car park.

Ron Morgan – Shrewsbury

My father taught there from 1964-1999. I am sure it was not wholly proper but on the days when you just could not get into the ground we would always end up 'popping into work'. As a very young lad I could stand on one of the very high stools, just about getting my eyes to the window height. It was from such an uncomfortable position that I saw the win over Exeter to gain promotion in 1979, and most of the cup run that year.

They say that your school years are the best of your life. I have stood on the Wakeman End several times on trips back to Shrewsbury and often looked up at those windows with a huge sense of sentimentality. The school and the ground have a place in my history.

Mark Evitts – Benington, Herts

Like many others, I was always fond of night matches at Gay Meadow. I have been to many grounds and stadiums, but leaving my spot on the Riverside, walking along the Wakeman Terrace with the Wakeman School to my right, and through those exit gates was always a joy regardless if Town won, lost or drew.

S. Laws – Shrewsbury

Being a Town fan was like being in a special club that only those who went knew about. On leaving the ground and walking up the Narrows, be it people moaning at a lost game or singing the name of someone like Squire Maguire, walking back into civilisation was an experience to behold.

Many times I used to look at the faces of drivers waiting at the traffic lights staring at us in our blue and amber scarves, probably wondering if the game was good or not.

Tim Unwin – Ellesmere

We all used to huddle together like sheep being shepherded out onto the fields from our pens when we left Gay Meadow. There is no way that I can recall the amount of times when we had lost and I used to turn around and swear at the ground, only to be there the next week and witness a great victory.

Diana Greene – Newtown

Boxing Day 1962 was when Town entertained local rivals Wrexham. The match finished with a scoreline of 4-2 in the Town's favour, it is absolutely certain that the game should never have been allowed to finish. The snow was so heavy during the second half the players and fans could hardly see the lines on the pitch and sometimes we didn't know if the ball was out or not.

I had sat with my grandad Sam Powell in the Directors Box that day and after the game he would talk with his pals, whilst I waited for him downstairs.

I can picture it now, the snow got heavier and after about an hour grandad came down the stairs and to his amazement the snow was several inches deep. It took us some time to walk home to the Old Post Office in Milk Street, Wyle Cop was always a steep climb and in those conditions somewhat treacherous.

This day was the beginning of the 'big freeze' and Town did not play again until the 21st February – six weeks without football at Gay Meadow.

Chris Smith – Telford

At a home game against Peterborough United in 1977 I think, it started hailing. The hail was the size of golf balls. There was only about 2,500 at the game to start off with and when the weather got so bad, everyone moved from the Tech End on to the Riverside. The funny thing was that when Jimmy Lindsay had a wayward shot, the ball ended up in the Tech End which resulted in the opposing goalkeeper having to climb over the wall and get the ball because no one else would!

Richard Owen Roberts – Tywyn, Gwynedd

You think it is a grotty place the first time you go, but then as your memories grow you learn to love the place.

Gary Howorth – Wirral

My father watched the transition from Midland League football in 1946 to a side who could take on Everton in 1962. For a while it looked like the momentous events at the Meadow I was going to see was the return to non-league football, while still beating Everton. Fortunately that was a one season aberration and Town's place in the league has since been reclaimed.

For me it will be the little events that I shall remember. The Bury player who turned around angrily to find he had been hit on the back of the neck by a catkin from the Riverside trees. My son's first visit to the Riverside toilets and asking where he could wash his hands. Most of all I shall miss the feeling of being home. It may have been past its best twenty years ago but it was our Gay Meadow, my Gay Meadow, the Meadow of my father and grandfather.

A ground to be rightly proud of.

Peter Taylor – Bristol

I have been going to the Gay Meadow for years. It is in my blood. Fans have always commented about the Riverside toilets, but recently at one night game the stench was near unbearable. There was a very pleasant looking girl standing with her boyfriend. I would have moved in and asked her who her favourite player was if not for the lucky chap standing next to her. Instead of edging towards the pitch she stayed near the toilet entrance. "How could an upstanding female stand such a stench?" I thought. I guess she must have loved the Town as much as me. I certainly won't miss that smell, that's for sure!

Andy Poole – Church Stretton

I have watched so many matches from my spot and I am something of a novice compared to some of the old stagers in the crowd! It will be heartbreaking to walk away from the Riverside, and the Meadow for the final time never to return.

Chris Czora – Shrewsbury

I moved to Shrewsbury in February 1989 aged 12. Having loved football for a number of years I had never really felt any real affinity for a particular team. I was utterly gobsmacked that this quiet little market town were entertaining the likes of Chelsea in the League. I knew straight away that this was the team for me! The uncle of my next door neighbour where we previously lived in Derbyshire was called Mark Hughes. He was a professional footballer who had played in the late seventies and early eighties for teams such as Manchester United and Everton, and was winding down his career playing for Stoke in what was known at the time as the Second Division. Having given his brother and nephew three complimentary tickets I was invited along.

Soon after taking our seats in the Station Stand, I watched a young Michael Brown skip down the right wing in front of us, whip in a cross and after no more than two minutes it was 1-0. I rose up from my seat to cheer, only to realise from the faces of the Stoke fans all around, that to punch the air might not be such a good idea, even for a 12 year old. I sat down quickly with a barely concealed smile on my face!

Of course, the records show that Town lost the game 1-2 but I did not actually remember such. I think it is a particular quirk of Shrewsbury fans, and certainly visitors to Gay Meadow to only remember the good times. The fact remains that there is so much wrong with Gay Meadow that it is incredible how much I love it. I will miss that ramshackle collection of rusting metal, cracked concrete, vegetated terraces and unique toilets.

You cannot put a price on character. If you could, Gay Meadow would be the most expensive football ground in the world!

Dave Beighton – Leeds

Things like getting excited when Father Christmas has been makes your childhood. But I have never seen my son so excited and still talk a month after the time we went into the Centre Stand, and he touched some of the players as they came out of the tunnel.

S. Evans – Shrewsbury

And then Ryan says, "Ladies and Gentlemen, Shrewsbury Town" and the lads run out to 'Catch Us If You Can.' Everybody unites and cheers as they come on to the pitch.

Henry Griffiths – Shawbury

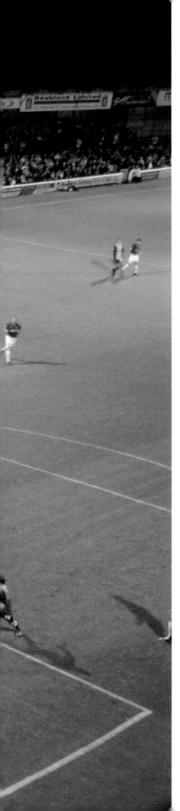

One of the great things about standing on the Riverside is the flexibility of walking all the way around two sides of the ground. Whatever kind of atmosphere you want, you can probably get it somewhere on the terrace.

I think we will all miss being able to gather behind the Wakeman End goal with five minutes to go, although this means that the Riverside often appears empty towards the end. It is always great if you arrive in time for a last minute winner!

Tom Leather – Oswestry

As a Walsall fan but also a fan of football in general, I have driven many times to watch a game after work at Gay Meadow. Sadly I was too young to go to the game where the record attendance was set, but I am proud Walsall feature in the record books at Gay Meadow. We all made fun of the coracle man and the floods, but that was Shrewsbury Town. I used to call it 'Shrewsbury Drown' when the flood pictures made the papers, but it was a great place and I will sincerely miss your ground. Where else could you watch a game of football in such fantastic surroundings with your back leaning against some rusty metal with ivy growing through it?

Danny Graham – Walsall

I always like to drive through the town centre on a match day. Maybe a train full of fans will be leaving the station as you go up the hill, then the further you get more and more football colours can be seen.

I park at St. Julian's Friars and see the ground under lights which is always best as I walk over the English Bridge. If the wind is blowing and you are late, you can usually hear the teams being read out from the other side of the bridge, but can't quite make out the names – so frustrating!

Passing through the Narrows and going by the programme sellers, golden gamble tickets and maybe a fanzine or two before the turnstiles, queuing for the season ticket turnstile when the others have no queue always brings a grumble, especially if you catch the five to three rush.

Tom Leather – Oswestry

Having passed my 11+ the choice of school was the Priory or Wakeman, and to a football fan this was a no-brainer with the Wakeman being right next to Gay Meadow, so in September 1964 I entered the Wakeman School.

Mr Derry was my music teacher and in one of his early lessons he was asking pupils about their prowess with instruments, he got to me and asked, "What do you play Smith?" I said, "Football, Sir!" and was banished to the back of the class.

Chris Smith – Telford

In the 1960s, often at half-time there would be charity collections. This was done by four or five people walking around the touchline holding a stretched out blanket into which fans threw coins. There were one or two injuries as you can imagine! But the folk who really put themselves at risk were the local press photographers who used to sit on their camera boxes just to the side of the goal post. One or two became victims of rocket shots and over lengthy sliding tackles!

John Ryan – Aberdeen

On a cold night at the Wakeman End I was taking pictures for the match day programme. Michael Brown sped down the wing and crossed the ball. I know it didn't result in a goal as I didn't hear the crowd cheer. All I can remember was myself and Browny ending up in a heap looking up at the floodlights. I think I was more shocked when I saw his stud marks on the metal box that I had been sitting on.

Thanks to Ian Woan, I now know what my orbital bone is. Woan apparently tackled a Bristol Rovers player and whacked the ball out for a throw in, which resulted in it hitting me! However, I was not looking at him at the time and the force of the ball pushed my camera into my face. Once again I was looking up at the floodlights in a daze. Four hours in hospital and two x-rays later, the doctors could not pinpoint what was causing my pain. After a much quicker examination by physio Simon Shakeshaft, he sent me back to hospital with his instructions, where I discovered I had broken my orbital.

Matthew Ashton – Shrewsbury

August 1978, 'Grease' was the big box office hit of the year, with John Travolta and Olivia Newton John spending most of the summer at number one with 'Summer Nights.' Punk was evolving into New Wave with bands like The Jam beginning to take on the mantle as pioneers of both music and fashion. Grange Hill was seen on our screens for the first time, and Maggie Thatcher was still only Leader of the Opposition.

On the afternoon of August 21st 1978, if you had asked me who I supported I would probably have said Liverpool. Although born in Shrewsbury and had lived there on and off for a couple of years, I had spent nearly fourteen years away from Shropshire, returning in the spring of 1978. While aware of Town, I was hardly a supporter.

But on that Tuesday in August a friend had suggested we go and watch them, and being at a loose end (school holidays) it seemed like a good idea. I decided to take my camera along to the game, a recent birthday present and a relatively new hobby at the time – at least if the football wasn't worth watching it was an opportunity to take some photographs. Such was the mindset with which I approached the game.

It was Stockport County, in the League Cup. I don't remember a great deal about the game, oddly, but I remember being there. We stood on the small piece of terracing that used to be in front of the old wooden Station Stand, next to the two or three hundred Stockport supporters.

Town won 1-0, although the abiding memory was less of Steve Biggins scoring than of the Stockport fans singing "Old Man, Old Man," at the grey-haired Ken Mulhearn.

As I left the Meadow I became increasingly aware that something had changed. There's an old cliché about not choosing your club, but your club choosing you – perhaps it was that. But what I did know as I walked home on that evening back in August 1978 was that I was no longer a Liverpool supporter, I had come home. My team, my club had become a reality and there was a very tangible realisation that there was no going back.

And so here we are nearly 30 years later. I will miss Gay Meadow. For all those years I have felt that same belonging, and the walk up the Narrows has become a ritual to which I look forward to each week. Much else has changed in my life over those years – work, marriage, fatherhood – but the one constant in all that time has been walking into the Meadow to see Shrewsbury Town. My Shrewsbury Town. There will always be a part of me that misses the old Meadow. Like losing a faithful labrador, you still expect to see him sitting by the gate, lying by the sofa, always there. And then, one day, no longer there. Just a memory. Just a photograph.

Paul Knapton – Edinburgh

We arrived in Shrewsbury in the summer of 2000, just after the great escape at Exeter. I started watching Town occasionally over the next few years and when we were drawn at home in the FA Cup Third Round to Everton, our ten year old son Daniel was keen to go to the game. Tickets were sold on a Sunday morning and due to the high demand we arrived at 6am to join the queue which was snaking its way back from Gay Meadow.

We were at the back of the English Bridge on a cold December's morning. The queue turned out to be a pleasant occasion, plenty of banter and the anticipation of getting tickets. I think everyone in the queue got tickets.

Following the monumental defeat of Everton and the home draw against Chelsea, plans began for the next night of queuing. Much debate was had about the time to set alarms. This time Daniel and I arrived before 4am to be greeted by a massive queue, which we joined by the Nags Head. Not much later it stretched to the Market Square. This experience was quite surreal, to be in Shrewsbury in the middle of the night, queuing with thousands of Town fans.

Many had set up stalls at pub closing time the previous night and continued an all night street party. Many were well supplied with flasks of hot drinks, tins of beer, chairs and other provisions. The time passed quite quickly with plenty of chat and humour, though there was anxiety connected to the size of the queue and the number of tickets available. I think the ticket office opened a bit early to get things moving, and to probably get the huge but orderly queue off the streets.

As we inched down the Wyle Cop and over the English Bridge, slowly towards the ground, speculation about the number of tickets left was rife. Jubilant fans walked by clutching their tickets, some reassuringly saying, "There's loads left," or others more worryingly, "They're down to the last 200." Where would the cut off point come?

The mixture of excitement and fear was almost worse than having a penalty in the last minute to win a vital game. Thankfully, we were in the last fifty or so that got tickets. Many were disappointed and some very frustrated, not suprisingly after all their efforts. I think the queuing experience has left a lasting memory equal to the football.

Thank God we didn't win and get Arsenal at home!

Patrick and Daniel Tomlinson – Shrewsbury

We packed the deckchairs and went down to the ground. We could not believe the scene at the Meadow. It was surreal to watch daybreak sat in a deckchair on the English Bridge where we joined the queue. All this for a football match!

For breakfast I nipped to the kebab shop under the railway bridge and got chips whilst the others saved my place. The owner had stayed open and was selling chips to queueing fans.

The queue started moving and it was apparent that the people who were first in line had made a night of it. There was an abandoned gazebo, cans and bottles of beer everywhere. By 9am I was back in bed, without any sleep, but with a ticket!

Chris Czora – Shrewsbury

After Shrewsbury drew with Wolves in the FA Cup Quarter Final, the replay was the following Tuesday. This meant the replay tickets went on sale the next day (Sunday morning). I was working at 9am so I got up early at 6.30 to get in the queue. To my horror it was well over the English Bridge, I finally got to the end of it half way up Wyle Cop. Yes, you guessed it, I was late for work, but there was no way I was going to miss that replay!

Glyn Young – Shrewsbury

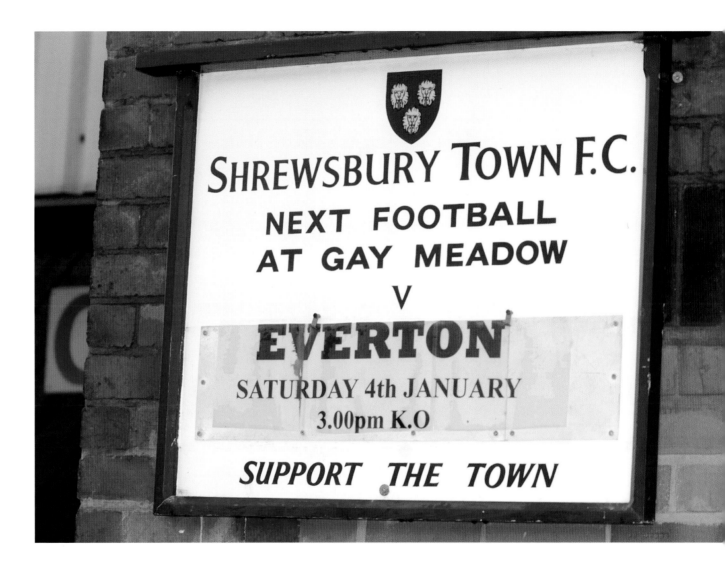

SHREWSBURY TOWN F.C.
NEXT FOOTBALL
AT GAY MEADOW
V
EVERTON
SATURDAY 4th JANUARY
3.00pm K.O
SUPPORT THE TOWN

I first went to Gay Meadow in 1948 when I was 11 years old. My father used to take me and I sat on the wall behind the goal at the Railway End, that was when we were allowed to sit on walls. It did not matter what the weather was like, the game was always played. I was very proud as when I was about 15 years old, I used to babysit for Bobby Brown. He was one of the Town's great players along with winger Martin Regan. When I got married in October 1959, Shrewsbury were playing Swindon Town. My husband's youngest brother was not going to miss that, so he got a doggy bag from the reception and took it to the match. It will be sad to see the Gay Meadow go, but good luck for a happy and successful time at the New Meadow.

Mooneen Williams – Wednesbury, West Midlands

I love the warmth and closeness of the Gay Meadow crowd. I can still hear it and smell it. I shall miss it.

Jeffrey Burke – Shrewsbury

My first visit to Gay Meadow was as a seven year old lad in 1963, when my dad (Dick Thomas) took me to my first match. We kept going to the odd game, loved it, and in 1965 became regular supporters. Since that day at the beginning of the 65/66 season, I have missed only five league or cup games at the Meadow.

Most of them were in the company of my dad. Sadly dad died in August 1984, aged just 55 from a heart attack. One week later we were at home for the first game of the season against Crystal Palace, but I had an empty seat next to me. I was in tears for most of the game, but we scored four and ran out easy winners. For me a very poignant memory. I am sure there will be many tears at the last game against Grimsby Town.

How my dad would have loved to see the New Meadow.

Colin Thomas – Abermule, Mid Wales

My love of Shrewsbury Town started in Wiltshire in the early sixties, mysteriously passed on to me by my father, a proud Shropshire exile. Ironically he was never a great football fan. It took all my powers of persuasion to get him to take me to Gay Meadow during one of our annual visits to my uncle in Minsterley. Prior to this, I had had to content myself with tantalising glimpses of the floodlights as we drove to dad's family home in Edgmond.

The year was 1967 if I remember correctly, so was it Walsall, Middlesbrough or Watford that we went to see? No, it was none other than a reserve game against Kidderminster! You could walk around the three sides of the ground in those days and I cannot recall anyone else being there. It was almost as though the whole match had been staged for my benefit.

The result was a 0-3 defeat, but I didn't really care. I had finally got to see the greatest football ground in the world. Forty years on and following a 240 mile motorway trek, I still feel the same excitement as I walk along the Wakeman End terrace at 2pm on a Saturday.

Richard Griffiths – Herne Bay, Kent

The name Peter Wilson is not one that I was familiar with until November 2005 and a perfectly normal visit to Gay Meadow. I turned up about an hour before the game and as usual I had read the programme. There were a fair few supporters already in the ground, all taking their places and chatting about the match. Some of the Mansfield Town players came out onto the pitch with their trainer and got a little round of applause from the visiting fans. I looked up and saw them start to warm up and then went back to whatever I was reading.

I don't know how long I had read for or what it was that distracted me but I found myself looking at a figure lying down in the Station End penalty area. Immediately I wondered what had happened, had he turned his ankle and just gone over? Was he just messing about? I had no idea what was going on. I looked at the faces of the players with him, they looked as perplexed as me but they also looked alarmed and concerned. One or two stewards were arriving quickly to see if they could help. Frantic expressions were exchanged as more people arrived to see if they could help.

Things were moving fast and it seemed as if the whole crowd were now watching as this upsetting scene unfolded. CPR was being given to the poor man and that told me how desperate the situation was. People from both sides were working together to try to save him but resuscitation rates are low outside hospital and this occasion was no different.

The game was cancelled as a mark of respect for Mr Wilson, which was the right decision. I remember feeling sorry for his partner who had probably seen him off expecting to see him later, but wouldn't.

It does not seem right for people to die a football match but it happens and they should be remembered.

Marcus Braddock – Shrewsbury

How many matches can there have been called off due to a death on the pitch? And all this before the game had even started.

I had already been down to the Gay Meadow to buy a programme and returned to The Globe to enjoy a pre-match pint with my mates and to read the programme. Suddenly messages and rumours started to emanate about a problem at the ground, until it was confirmed that the Mansfield goalkeeping coach had suffered a heart attack and worse still, had died.

The game was off and we spent the rest of that Saturday afternoon in The Globe having our own wake and coming to terms that there are more important things in life than football.

Colin James – Wistanstow

Perhaps one of the most haunting moment was against Mansfield, when having just arrived at our usual spot in the Riverside, we were told the match was cancelled. It was a horrible moment and very eerie leaving the ground and getting a ticket for the replay.

As we left there were people coming in and we had to stop hundreds of them and tell them the sad news – many did not believe us.

Getting home to hear that he had died was a very sad moment.

Peter Horton – Shrewsbury

After taking my son and daughter to the World Cup in Germany and seeing all the amazing stadiums, driving back through France and stopping off in Paris to see the Stade de France, I made sure we visited Gay Meadow before it was knocked down as I wanted them to see what football grounds with terraces used to be like.

After a trip to Blists Hill Victorian Town Museum we came to a home game . My daughter wondered if Shrewsbury Town was connected with the Ironbridge Gorge Museum and called it a 'living football stadium museum' because she thought it was so old and un-modern.

Gary Teddington – Warwick

I was about five or six when I went to my first Gay Meadow match with my dad some 35 or so years ago. We sat in the stands and drew 0-0 and it was very very boring. Unsurprisingly after this initial disappointment I decided to support Liverpool instead as they at least looked like they knew what they were doing!

I went a couple more times with my uncle and we stood on the Riverside. I remember him lifting me up so I could stand on some rails against the metal at the back of the stand. I hung on for dear life as it seemed to be quite some way up for a six year old lad.

This must have been when the hard core were in the Station End. I can remember the hooligan element at that time - my uncle called them the 'Bovver Boys' – taunting the away supporters with songs like 'A-G... A-G-R... A-G-R-O... Agro' and, 'Come and have a go a the Station End Agro' or that's what it sounded like to my innocent little ears stood on the Riverside. It all seemed much more exciting and noisy standing on a terrace rather than sitting in a stand.

Vince Jones – Martinstown, Dorset

At the age of twelve I started to want to go and watch Shrewsbury Town at the Gay Meadow after hearing reports of them on Beacon Radio with Mike Jones from places like Huddersfield Town.

Hearing the name Shrewsbury associated with other towns and cities on the radio made me proud of where I lived and I wanted to be a part of it.

My uncles were mad on football but were all spending time away at a family wedding in Australia. My father didn't want to take me, however he would not let me attend on my own. I was in tears when he would not take me, insisting that I paid for my own entrance in trying to quash my enthusiasm.

However the next week we played Charlton Athletic I think. Anyway I had saved up enough pocket money and insisted to my father that I went to Gay Meadow. I loved it. I was stood with men smoking pipes, men swearing openly to the players in front of them and other youngsters like myself.

I remember Paul Johnson was the left back and his cross was met by one of our strikers who ballooned the ball over the bar into the Abbey Gardens. I looked over my head on the Wakeman End and for the first time in life felt a complete injustice when I saw a supporter watching from the trees with what must have been a superb panoramic view overlooking the paying fans.

I later went on the Riverside when my uncles returned and grew from a boy to a man on there. When my father passed away one of them told me that he had felt he had been a bad father for not letting me follow my passion.

Dad if you are reading this, with you as my father and with my visits to Gay Meadow, this meant my up bringing was the best I could have ever wished for.

Danny Jones – Wellington

When I was about six (1968) we moved from Harlescott Grange to Cherry Orchard and the big boys used to take us on trips to the Gay Meadow which involved climbing the drainpipe behind the Tech End toilets and bunking over the wall into the game. Then we used to congregate on the Station End, although I remember very little about the games.

One week the club had daubed the drainpipe with a sticky anti-climb paint which I didn't like, but the big lads told me to get on with it. It got on my clothes and if it is any consolation, it put me off bunking in again.

Adrian Farmer – Shrewsbury

I remember a little guy with one front tooth who was tucked away every game at the back of the Riverside. He was an ever present fixture and you could find him dressed in an old overcoat leaning against the corrugated wall. What made him so special to me was the bugle that he occasionally sounded throughout the match and the constant smile that he wore for every game, every week.

In contrast to this little guy was 'Roman Nose' so called for the obvious reason. He could be found behind the Station End goal every match. He was always dressed in a grubby flowing overcoat and a shirt in need of a wash. He was there in all weathers yelling at the top of his voice – most of which is unprintable. Needless to say my dad wasn't too keen on me getting too close to the man with the Roman nose but he was a fascinating attraction to the loads of kids who gravitated to him for those ninety minutes.

Vince Jones – Martinstown, Dorset

There were a few characters amongst the Town supporters. One I especially remember was a middle-aged guy called Raymond. Raymond, who had a distinctive Roman nose, always stood behind the Station End goal.

If someone shouted a comment towards the pitch, Raymond inevitably repeated it, but twice as loud. Hence the nickname 'Parrot'.

John Ryan – Aberdeen

One of the great things about the Meadow has been witnessing the antics of some of the characters who frequented the terraces, especially when there has been a dearth in the on field entertainment.

One bloke (who sadly is no longer with us) sticks out. His name was Terry Roberts, although he was lovingly known as 'Anti-Tank' to everyone at SY2 6AB. Anti-Tank was the biggest berater of match officials I have ever known. His favourite line, delivered at about 100 decibels was "Referee you're a shit-house". One game, for a laugh, me and a mate stood near him to count the number of times he said this phrase. I think it was nearly thirty!

One game early on in a season I remember him a bit worse for wear (as he usually was to be fair) in the Wakeman End. I think he must have been holiday because he had a tan and tourist type T-shirt with 'Cyprus' on it. He was also wearing a fetching Fez hat. He spent the first half of the game wildly clapping his hands and bellowing "Come on Cyprus" to the bemusement of fans and players alike.

He died in 1994, he must of been in his late forties I think. The Club had heard and there was a minutes' silence dedicated to him before kick-off. Whilst at first it was observed, people then spontaneously started clapping and then started singing "Anti-Tank, Anti-Tank, Anti-Tank". Some people might have thought that it was a bit disrespectful to do this, but given the man himself was never quiet for long when he was in the Meadow it somehow seemed appropriate to me.

At his funeral, someone I knew who went told me there was nearly 400 people in attendance. He must have made some good friends down the Meadow over the years.

Normally you would say 'Rest in Peace Anti-Tank' but I don't think he knew the meaning of the word rest!

Tim Gallon – Selly Oak, Birmingham

Anti-Tank was such a colourful character. He made the crowd part as he ran to the front to scream at the top of his voice at opposing goalkeepers. My friend in the stand always said he could hear him sitting in the main stand.

He was worth the entrance fee alone. He was so funny and passionate. I don't think I ever saw him get into trouble and he was considered part of the furniture, just like the coracle which as a youngster I thought was the norm.

Another fan we are proud of is a man called Monty. I don't know him personally but I believe he walks from his home town of Montgomery to Shrewsbury to watch the matches.

I now sit in the stand, but for the last few games I stood up and it made my day when I saw Monty. I am glad he is still around.

H. Collins – Shrewsbury

I was at one match when Anti-Tank was being rather loud and rowdy, obviously fuelled by drink, but the crowd were enjoying his antics and all around were in good humour. All of a sudden two police officers emerged and tried to escort him out of the ground. Suddenly the mood of the Wakeman End changed, the police got booed and the fans refused to make way for the police to guide Anti-Tank away and out of the ground.

Being mature, I approached the police officers and asked why they were doing this. I pointed out he was a local character and fondly liked by all Town fans, who accepted his antics in good nature. They told me it was for anti-social behaviour and basically to mind my own business. Because the police officers were intent on ejecting Anti-Tank from the Gay Meadow, I asked for their names and numbers and said that if the Wakeman End crowd did react violently to their antics then I would report them to the Chief Constable, as being instigators of the trouble.

With that they told Anti-Tank to behave himself and return to his place in the Wakeman End. Unfortunately for me the two police officers stood either side of me, both glaring at me, until the end of the game.

Colin James – Wistanstow

My father passed away recently, but at the funeral all the pain turned to laughter as I recalled a story about him trying to stop me tell the careers teacher that I wanted to be a turnstile operator at Gay Meadow. Thankfully for him, I never did achieve my dream job!

H. Preston – Bayston Hill, Shrewsbury

Every time I go a match, I promise myself not to buy the Golden Gamble. My wife stopped me playing the lottery but after some chap next to me in the Wakeman Stand scooped about 700 quid, I could not stop buying the tickets!

Sam Davies – Telford

Recollections about particularly important games, favourite players and the fans' personal stories associated with them will be numerous I am sure. But as Town fans we also have a sense, an inheritance perhaps, of the collective memories that will outlive the Gay Meadow itself. Many decades of activities on the turf and the mud, will survive like newsreel ghosts. In this sense the Meadow will survive.

For every generation of supporter there will be countless memories to conjure. As a community we share a unique collection of experiences. Saying goodbye to the Gay Meadow may feel like a death in the family, and we shall miss the old ground for certain – but if we miss someone special to us we can be thankful for the experiences we shared and celebrate their contribution to our own lives.

So, in saying goodbye, we must celebrate the memories we share, and anticipate many more memories to come at the new ground.

Geoff Hands – Brighton

I'm sure that I will go down to the New Meadow once in a while, but sitting down is probably the final straw for me. I'll always be a Town fan, but I'm sure that I'll always talk about 'the good old days' when there was 17,000 standing up, rather than the 'super' new era in 2007 when we all have to sit down. I guess we will never again have the sight of hundreds of Birmingham City fans sitting on the grass between the goal line and the terrace, on the wall or fencing. The crushes that happened several times a game on the Riverside when anything exciting happened. Dangerous? Maybe. Exciting? Without doubt.

Yes I would rather slum it standing up on a draughty terrace with highly dubious facilities.

Dave Poulter – Shrewsbury

I have been a 'Riversider' for as long as I have been a Town fan, my brother has claimed his space for over 35 years and normally saves me a bit. I normally wear an old Town shirt, I have a collection from over the years and so I can pick from 20 years worth. I have lost my glasses a few times when rushing to the front, but it's always worth it when we have scored. I never like to be behind the goal as you miss too much action at the other end.

Darren De Banks – St. Albans

59

I always heard about the new signings and rumours from those claiming to be in the know standing near me on the Riverside, but I could never believe people when after a flood they said the groundsman was watering the pitch three days later. Apparently the watering of the pitch was 100% true, however most of the signings that I heard about was a pack of lies as they never took place.

Russ Brown – Shrewsbury

With the sun setting and the sky turning the deepest blue it was all a bit too storybook. 'Catch Us If You Can' being played at the start of the second-half presumably for the last time was just making the significance build and build. And then full-time, and whilst it was not the perfect result, I honestly felt relieved that we at least did not wave goodbye to the Meadow with a bitter taste that always accompanies a defeat.

Yes I did stroll onto the pitch briefly, but then made my way back over the wall to my spot on the terrace again. I just stood there and tried to take it all in for what I knew would be the final time.

And when the stewards inevitably came and ushered out the last few of us I will honestly never forget the moment when I left that spot. I know it sounds ridiculous but I actually clung on to the barrier with my hands and when I let go and walked away... well some of you will understand!

But it was obvious that to me and so many others it was a very special and cherished place.

If at some point in the future another ground with three sides framed by trees, a castle overlooking it and a river at its side becomes a venue for league football then maybe the Meadow's passing will not be so hard to take. But we all know that this could never happen as neither the setting nor the memories of Gay Meadow could ever be reproduced anywhere else.

Put simply, Gay Meadow was, and will, always remain in our hearts as being quite unique from any other football ground. Let's just be thankful that we were amongst the lucky ones who witnessed it in its glory, no matter how dilapidated such glory may have been!

Paul Gladwell – Edinburgh

The views from the Family Stand were fantastic, despite the posts holding up the roof. To this day I do not know why I watched from the Riverside when I grew up.

John Rutherford – Craven Arms

Few grounds are as picturesque as Gay Meadow. The Abbey peering over the edge of the ground, the fine trees stretching over the Riverside and Shrewsbury Castle peeping out from behind the Station End.

When you are at the Meadow, you are in Shrewsbury.

Season 2006-07 has been great as I have come to appreciate the ground and make every moment count.

Gay Meadow – rest in peace, and thank you for the many memories, happy and sad, that you have given me.

Chris Czora – Shrewsbury

The location of the Meadow has much to do with the unique, idyllic and homely qualities which supporters cherish. From the stands you are overlooked by the buildings which line the steep ascent of Wyle Cop and Town Walls as well as the RSI.

From the Riverside you can see the over 900 year old Abbey silently standing guard and the trains passing the ground as they roll into the station.

You can see the statue of Viscount Hill, from which many speculative effort has rebounded to be met with amusement and disbelief of Town fans! From the Wakeman End you have the prime view of Laura's Tower and the trees overhanging the River Severn, particularly idyllic in the early and late season.

Gay Meadow was certainly a football ground like no other – and etched in character, history and tradition.

Nick Statham – Shrewsbury

The Meadow has been a sturdy home for a hardy bunch of fans, who have deserved better than the team has shown season after season. But that makes leaving all the more hard in my eyes. I felt comfortable with the fact that we were a team doing nothing scrapping around the lower echelons of league football because, hell we had a lovely ground.

The freezing cold LDV game in October with 1,300 in and you and your mates huddled round a cup of hot chocolate wondering just why the hell we did it.

It will be a sad day when the bulldozers move in and destroy what has been a part of thousands upon thousands of Salopians heritage.

Glyn Price – Shrewsbury

What I will miss most about it will be the cold, wet winter afternoons, just like my very first game that my dad took me to as a 13 year old. Regardless of how the team played, the Meadow was what made it all that little bit better.

Daniel Purchase – Whitchurch

I will not miss coming out of Gay Meadow on a wet night after losing and then walking into one of the large puddles. That really seemed to sum up the evening for me!

Gary Howorth – Wirral

The ultimate present for a ten year old boy must be to be mascot for his favourite team. Thus one sunny autumn morning in the mid 1980s I awoke with the gleeful excitement for my one and only appearance on the hallowed Gay Meadow turf, only to look in the mirror to see my face dotted with chicken pox spots. Surely Chic Bates wouldn't allow his starting eleven to be exposed to the aforementioned contagious affliction. So it came to pass that I became the only striker in the history of Gay Meadow to hit a thunderous left foot volley past goalkeeper Steve Perks from eight yards whilst wearing his mother's concealer.

The day got more surreal when I was kidnapped by Brighton strikers Dean Saunders and Justin Fashanu who didn't have a mascot so made me wear a Brighton shirt!

Paddy Pringle – Leeds

I was mascot for the Town when we lost to Huddersfield in 1987. David Geddis scored. Having been a season ticket holder for many years before, running onto the pitch with Nigel Pearson was a dream come true. Scoring past Steve Perks as the team warmed up capped the whole experience. Weekly trips to Gay Meadow were a part of my youth. As a youngster I sat in the Centre Stand with my cousin Robert and in our teenage years we progressed to the Riverside.

Chris Hawkins – London

I had the great honour when I was ten of being Town's mascot for the day. We played Grimsby Town and won 4-1. I remember leading the team out with Nigel Pearson and although I was a bit nervous and starting to have second thoughts as the time approached, I couldn't have the Town skipper thinking I was a wimp, so I did as I was told and kicked the ball I had been given as far as I could onto the pitch.

From then on my nerves disappeared and I even enjoyed brief fame the following week at school for being the boy who had scored a penalty against Steve Perks.

Sadly a career as a professional footballer didn't follow, but a place remained in my heart for Shrewsbury Town.

Nick Statham – Shrewsbury

SHREWSBURY TOWN
F C
GOLDEN GAMBLE
WINNING NUMBER

6 8

FOR £800·00

I have got to know lots of people over the years to 'nod' to at Gay Meadow. The interesting thing is that if you meet them away from Gay Meadow they seem like best friends, but you don't know their names.

STFC and hence Gay Meadow is in my blood, I could not think of supporting anyone else. It's like a badge of honour to wear, you have to wear it no matter how low things get. I dislike the 'fair weather' support.

Gary Howorth – Wirral

Yes, people say it is old and dilapidated, but surely anyone can appreciate the unique setting and the beauty of the surroundings. In all my time of going to the Meadow, the ground has changed so little that even subtle changes would seem like a big deal to me. I was honestly upset when the huge Chuckie Chicken advertisement on the Station End roof was replaced.

Paul Gladwell – Edinburgh

My love affair with Shrewsbury Town started on my eleventh birthday, when a friend's father took us to the Gay Meadow on the steam train from Craven Arms to watch a 4-3 thriller against Port Vale.

My mate and I could hardly see over the wall at the Wakeman End and we got split up from his father and had to be reunited through a tannoy call. To this day I still have this programme, as I do from all the other games I watched in the subsequent 49 years.

Colin James – Wistanstow

PLEASE DO NOT STAND THIS SIDE OF BARRIER.
GANGWAY MUST BE KEPT TOTALLY
CLEAR AT ALL TIMES.

Over the years I have got to know most people around me, however I still hardly know their names. Also I stand quite close to one of my customers from work although I did not know that until recently. Being a Shrewsbury Town fan means everything to me. I support my local team, although that nearly did not happen as an old friend of mine from Junior School and his dad used to take me up to Anfield regularly. I am very pleased that I made the right choice. Having so many highs and lows is much better than watching a washing machine go round and round – ie Premiership Football.

David Ruscoe – Shrewsbury

It is the little quirks of watching from the terraces at the Meadow that are irreplaceable. The fans who hurtle themselves through the masses, down ten steps of terracing, to express their anger at how the linesman was neglecting his need for a visit to the opticians. And the way that no matter how perfectly I plan my standing position on the Riverside, I always somehow end up with my view of one goal, if not both, obscured by a beam.

Jonathan Guntrip – Shrewsbury

I was about eleven years old in the early sixties and was in the Royal Salop Infirmary recovering from a fractured skull, which initially had me fighting for my life. The pre-season friendlies were starting and I asked if the doctors would let me go to the match – they said absolutely not, bed rest only.

But the nurses knew how passionate I was about Salop, so they wrapped me up in a blanket, gave me pillows and wheeled me out onto the balcony to watch the match. The only trouble was I could only see the Tech End goal, so had to gauge from the crowd's reaction if anyone had scored at the Station End. We were playing Leicester City, a First Division team at the time, I seem to recall we won 4-2, but I might have been dreaming that, after all the doctor said I was lucky to be alive after such a smack on the head – so it could have been my imagination.

Ron Morgan – Shrewsbury

I first started going to the Meadow in 1968 taken to the ground with some friends by my father. We walked from Meole Estate and from the moment I got onto the Station End where all the noise was coming from, I knew this was the sport I wanted to be in some small way part of.

That was me then for a few years, watching Town from the spiritual homeland of Town's youth support, until September 1975 when Crystal Palace came to town.

At the time they were the league high fliers, managed by Malcolm Allison and having several nationally recognised players in their midst, most notably a young Peter Taylor. Palace brought with them a lot of noisy and aggressive support who gathered on the Wakeman End and Riverside. For whatever reason this seemed to stir the Town support on the Riverside like I'd never witnessed before, and elements of the home support began singing and chanting in opposition to the fans. This in turn led a mass migration from the Station End (in the days when you could walk around the ground) where most of the vocal support remained for the rest of the game.

Whether it was because the position at the centre of the Riverside offered better views of the pitch or because it was in closer proximity to visiting fans, I don't know, but the Station End appeared to die that day and the Riverside was born as the refuge of the Town's hardcore element.

Alan James – Shrewsbury

What I will miss most about Gay Meadow is the terracing. As a young Riversider I often used to stand in the centre just to the left of the buffet, and I used to love the surges after a Town goal. Once the celebrations had died down I would end up in a completely different position to where I was before the goal!

Dale Skitt – Telford

I have stood and sat in most parts of the ground. As a youngster I used to stand in front of the middle section of the Riverside but as I have got older I now sit in the Wakeman Stand, hopefully in seat S 82, if no one else gets to it first.

Even my wife who has been a supporter for three years misses the place when we are not playing over the summer.

Gay Meadow is such a special place. Many people, including myself, have grown up with the place in their hearts.

Gary Howarth – Wirral

Since I was fourteen I have always stood on the Riverside. To start with I stood down at the front, but for the last five seasons I have stood at the back near to where all the singing originates, as I like an atmosphere and join in with some of the songs.

I have also started to wear the same clothes for every match now as well (including STFC socks). I started to bring my mate along for the occasional match but after a few he was hooked and has come with me ever since. I find the Gay Meadow special for its location and for its looks as it is an old style ground. I had that flag made that held pride of place on the scaffolding for the final season at Gay Meadow.

David Ruscoe – Shrewsbury

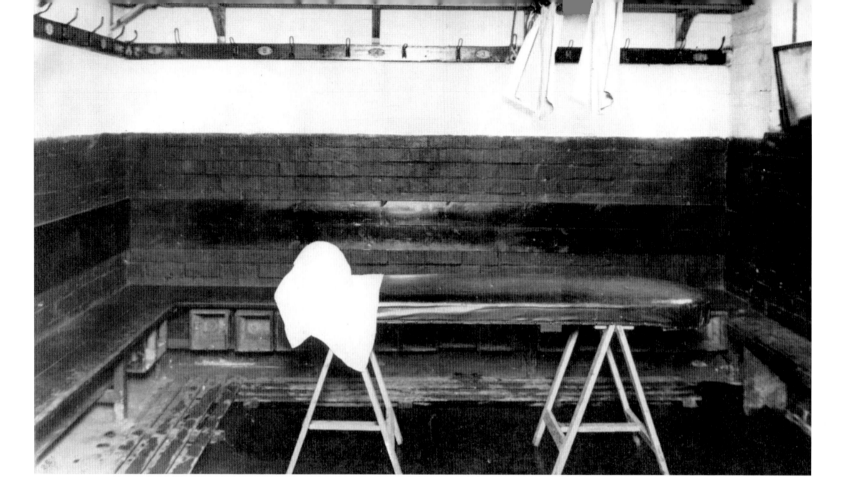

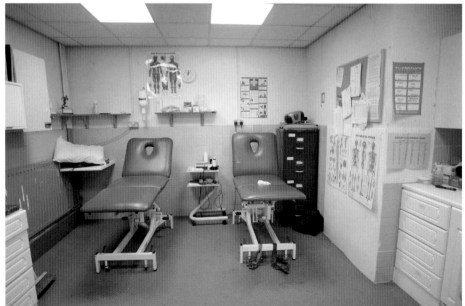

Midland Youth
Cup Final

Shrewsbury Town Youth
v
Walsall OR Grimsby

Bank Holiday
Monday 7th May 2007

At the Gay Meadow

6:00pm Kick Off

£3 adults
£1 children

Shrewsbury Town FC must have been proud of Lenny the Lion the day the Battle of the Mascots took place at Gay Meadow.

It was a wonderful event that I shall never forget. I think every rule in the football law book was broken that day, as the mascots from all over the country chased a huge football.

Claire Thomas – Telford

I must admit I used to go looking for trouble when I was in my youth, but since my daughter Charlotte was born I feel I have matured into a sensible father.

Out of all the hours and days that I have stood on the terraces, hand on heart, I don't think that I have smiled and laughed so much at the Meadow as when Charlotte was with me for the Battle of the Mascots.

It was a proud day for Shrewsbury Town to stage such an event.

The goal that Lenny the Lion scored at the Station End would rival any that I have seen by David Geddis or Carl Griffiths!

Willy Graham – Shrewsbury

The late Arthur Rowley scored a cracker of a goal against Bradford Park Avenue in the League in the early sixties. He was near the halfway line on the Riverside touchline and just let fly at the Station End goal. The keeper never moved. The legendary ex-Newcastle United goalkeeper Jimmy Scoular, then the Bradford boss, jumped out of the dugout in disbelief, holding his head in his hands! A disbelief that we all shared, having just witnessed something unbelievable.

The segregation of fans in those days was unheard of and unnecessary. Although there was the normal banter, home and visiting fans mixed on the terraces without the slightest hint of trouble. Indeed, if Town were kicking into the Station End for the first half, most of us would be behind the goal. At half-time we would make the trek along the Riverside terraces to the Tech End with the, usually smaller, crowd of visiting supporters doing the opposite.

I was at the game when the record attendance was set – over 18,000 for the League game against Walsall, at the end of the season. The Saddlers gained promotion that night and although there was nothing really for the Town to play for, apart from local pride, there was not any feeling of uneasiness even though Town and Walsall fans mixed together all over the ground.

John Ryan – Aberdeen

I would go over into the seated area for cup games, simply for the experience, but it lacked the passion and atmosphere that is often created on the Riverside.

There are some crazy people down the Meadow and I always end up in conversation with some pensioner, hearing stories of the 'good old days'.

Daniel Purchase – Whitchurch

At the Arsenal cup game I was not able to get my feet properly on the ground for half the match as there were so many more people in the ground. It was probably something to do with the ability to get into the Riverside through a hole in the stand!

Darren De Banks – St. Albans

It is so easy to get romantic about the Gay Meadow, but on the face of it, I think it had had its day.

Helen Perks – Shrewsbury

VISITING SUPPORTERS

SEASON TICKET HOLDERS
SUPPORTERS CLUB
MEMBERSHIP
TICKET HOLDERS

VISITORS STATION STAND

SENIOR CITIZENS / JUNIORS   ADULTS

£10   £15

13   14

As soon as I passed my driving test in 1972, I started supporting Shrewsbury Town. At that time I was living in a small village near Ludlow.

When my young son Steve was about five, he asked me to take him to a match, and since then he too has been hooked on the Town. A couple of years later, my daughter Shavorne also became an avid Town fan.

In 1991 we moved to Bridgnorth and continued to watch the Town. In 2002 my work took me to Greece for seven months and it cost me fortune keeping up with the scores via text.

When we had the dream draw against Chelsea I pleaded with my bosses to let me come home for two days, which they duly did and paid for my flights!

As you probably have seen, that was my Bridgnorth Shrews flag hanging on the Wakeman End floodlight pylon for the last month at the Meadow.

How ironic that it was my son Steve, who I took to the Meadow for his first game in the early 1980s, who climbed the floodlight on the night of the MK Dons game to take the flag down.

Not only was it an emotional night for me after 37 years of going to Gay Meadow but also for Steve, after 25 years.

D. Power – Bridgnorth

In November 1969 at an average Division Three game against Barrow, we were 0-1 down and the referee blew for full-time as Terry Harkin shot into the Barrow goal. All the players surrounded the referee as they left the pitch with no one in the crowd knowing whether we had equalised or not. Most of the 4,000 crowd remained behind to hear the final scores over the tannoy, and there was a massive cheer when we heard Shrewsbury 1 Barrow 1 being announced.

Richard Hobbs – Nottingham

Although it was not one of my favourite games, I will always remember the 11-2 victory over Marine in the FA Cup. At the time I lived in Huddersfield and travelled with another fan from Leeds. He used to drive but did not fancy the 100 plus mile round trip to watch a cup tie with a non-league minnow – but I decided to go anyway.

We started pretty badly and as the first half progressed no one would have expected us to rack up eleven goals during the next hour. I went behind the goal as our tenth seemed inevitable and I was very smug about the fact I could see myself on Match of The Day that night with my travelling companion still sat at home in Leeds!

That match influenced me in two ways. I then spent months going through the same turnstile in the hope of a repeat performance. Whenever I did not fancy the long trip to Gay Meadow on other Saturdays, I'd remind myself that if I didn't go then I might just miss a 'Marine-like' miracle.

Mike Exton – Cairo, Egypt

Specific moments for me would include my first game as a young lad when my brother and dad took me. I did not know any of the players or who the opposition were, and I remember wondering if I needed glasses to see. I remember it seemed huge walking into the ground having never been to anything like it before and the sheer number of people there was overwhelming.

Yet the atmosphere hooked me right away, and before the game had even kicked off I knew I wanted to win more than anything – a feeling that has never changed almost twenty years later.

Peter Horton – Shrewsbury

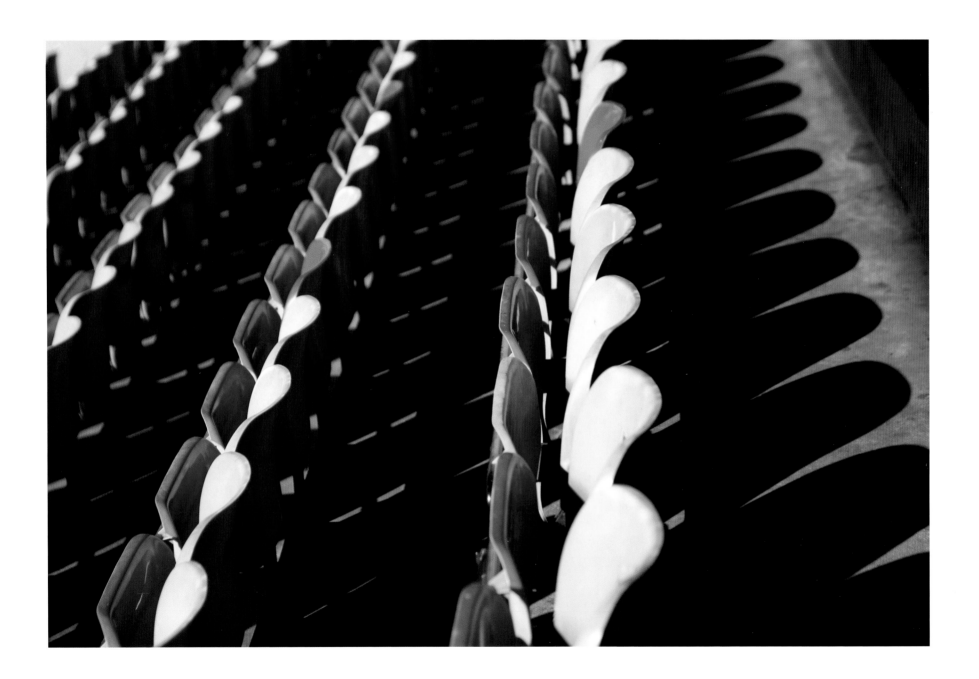

The first thing I remember was going to get my match ticket. There was a feeling of complete horror when I arrived at the Meadow to see a queue filling the pavement about five deep stretching up over the English Bridge. So I set off to join the back of it. A feeling of increasing anxiety arose as the queue snaked up Wyle Cop and round into Dogpole. Still it continued until I finally joined the back of it by St. Mary's Church.

A gang of lads walked past, laughing and saying "you'll never get a ticket". I felt aggrieved, because I hadn't missed a game all season and it didn't seem fair. Oh, the feeling of mounting anxiety as I got closer to the ground, down Wyle Cop at a shuffling pace. Shuffling and stopping, people complaining about others pushing in, over the English Bridge, round the corner towards the ground and ever closer to that ticket office.

Finally, almost able to touch it when someone says, "they are running out of tickets" – just another wind up - to the front of the queue, handing over my money and leaving clutching my ticket in a state of euphoria as if we'd just scored!

David Hawksworth – Birkenshaw, West Yorkshire

I was born in Shropshire, grew up in Market Drayton and now live in the North West. People wonder, since there are five Premiership clubs within a thirty mile radius of our home, and my husband was an avid Tranmere Rovers supporter, why should I want to spend money on train fare, and hang around Crewe Station on cold winter days, to go and support a League Two football team?

The answer has to be not so much that I want to, but that I NEED to.

There was a Shrewsbury Town shaped hole in my heart that only one football team could fill.

After years of being unable to go out at weekends due to family commitments, I suddenly decided in 2002, that I would go and support the team from the county of my birth. I went to my first match at the Gay Meadow in August 2003. That was it, I was hooked and hopelessly in love not with one man, but with eleven of course.

Not only was I in love with the team, but with the whole scenario, the excitement of the game, the spectacle of the spires of Shrewsbury rising up behind the trees on the Riverside, the friendliness of the supporters who made me so welcome.

Supporting Shrewsbury Town is like catching a bug that you cannot shake off. But the symptoms are usually so pleasant, you don't ever want to be cured.

Pauline Griffiths – Wigan

I was aged seven when I first went to see the Town at Gay Meadow with my dad and we sat in the Family Enclosure. Town beat Stoke City 4-1, Paul Tester coming on as sub and scoring. My childhood memories include going with my dad and grandad, then later with my mates on the Riverside.

Later still I took my wife and son, who went to his first game against Peterborough United on Friday March 16th 2007, aged three.

Paul Davies – Welwyn Garden City, Herts

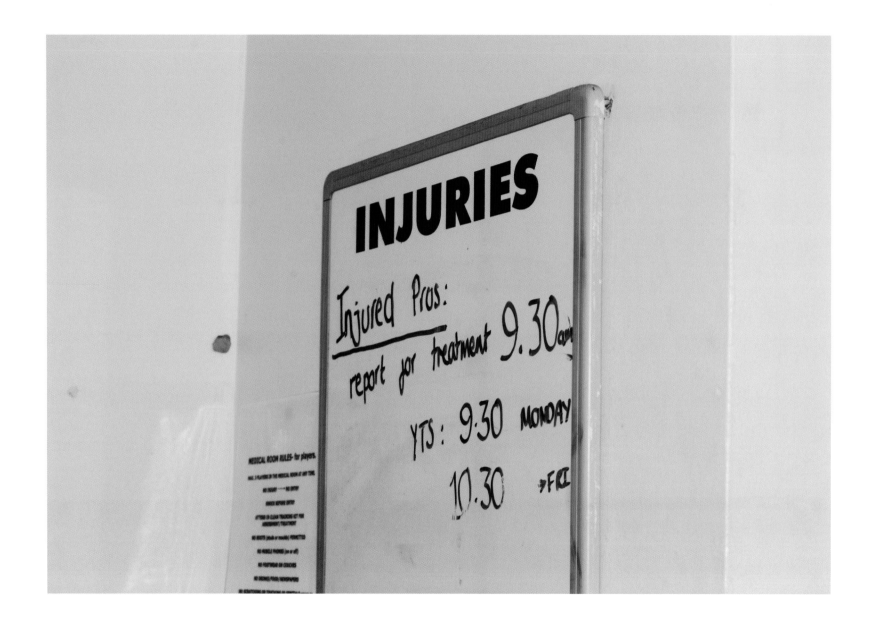

111

As a thirteen year old on a wet winter Saturday afternoon, my dad took me to watch my very first game at the Meadow, it was against Southend. We stood on the Riverside and that is where I got my season ticket for the next year. I remember Luke Rodgers tearing apart the Southend defence and goals from Rioch and Jemson gave us a 2-0 win. From that day on I never wanted to spend my Saturdays any other way.

Daniel Purchase – Whitchurch

The strange thing about Gay Meadow is that in thirty years of supporting the Town, I have never lived within 150 miles of it. And yet it has been home to my happiest memories. It is somewhere that literally felt like a heaven to me every time I went there.

Paul Gladwell – Edinburgh

During my last visit in January 2007 against Hartlepool, I remember looking around the Meadow, staring at the terracing, the surrounding trees, the school, the railway, the castle and the River Severn.

I found it hard to believe that I would never be here again, a large part of my life, home to the greatest team in my heart and some would say my second home. I then turned and began the long journey home with a tear in my eye, but with great pride. Thanks for the memories.

Andrew David Hill – Rosenberg, Texas, USA

When I was a member of the 1st Monkmoor Cub Scouts and on Bob-a-Job week, the whole pack got to sweep the terraces. This was a great thrill to us as the TV were there to film the whole thing and that evening my whole family were glued to the TV to see me with a brush in my hand sweeping away.

I am now a season ticket holder and despite moving away from the town, you will still find me behind the goal at the Wakeman End cheering on the 'Mighty Shrews' with my son.

I will miss Gay Meadow and am not really looking forward to sitting down to watch a match, but things have to move on.

Tony Wellings – Preston

I used to go with my cousin Brian to the football. We stood on the halfway line on the Riverside, me with a fat rattle (remember them?) and Brian had a big handbell which he used to ring like hell when Arthur Rowley scored. As I grew older and in my teens, I progressed to the Station End and we were then known as the 'Station End Boot Boys' – no aggro just lots of noise from us back heeling the old corrugated steel panels that used to serve as the back wall.

In my grown up times I progressed to the Wakeman Stand and then after my son came along, the Centre Stand until I became a steward and I now sit at Gate 8, Station End.

It is sad that Gay Meadow must go, but that is progress and we all as loyal supporters should thank the forward thinking directors for the wonderful place that will be New Meadow.

Len Crane – Shrewsbury

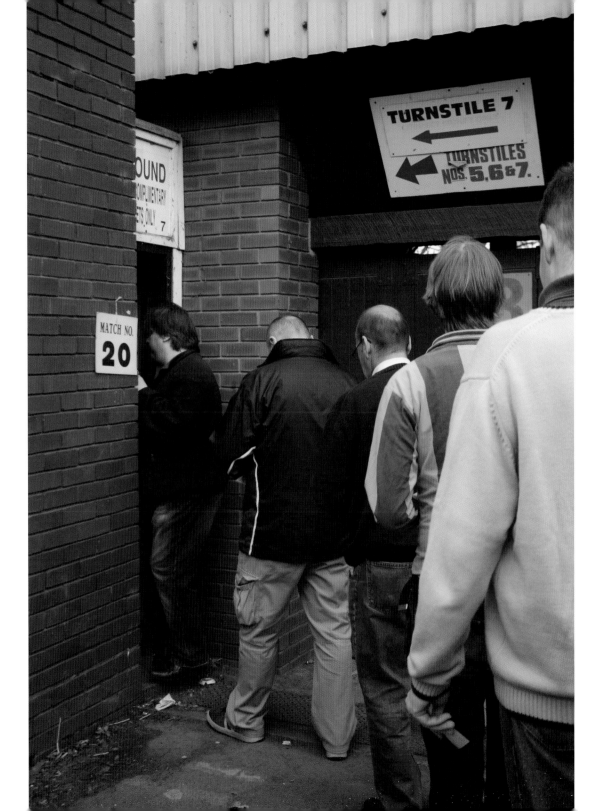

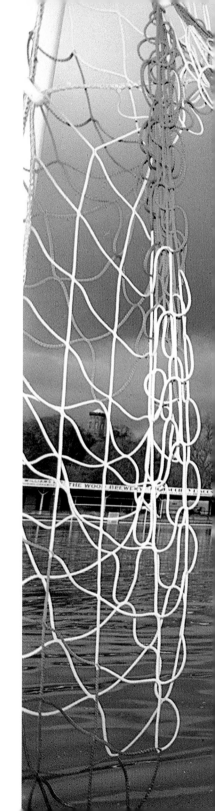

In the sixties, crowd trouble was not unheard of. The car park behind the Station End was just a cinder surface in those days. Following a draw with Arsenal in the FA Cup, a load of stones and cinders were hurled from the car park, over the Station End terracing roof and onto the fans, by, we assume disgruntled Gooners – who should have really been happy that they were going away with a draw!

John Ryan – Aberdeen

After our exploits against Chelsea, Leeds and Manchester City in previous years, we were confident of an upset. I was thirteen and it was a tremendous occasion being at the game. I was an avid 'Station Ender' so was rather put out when the police in their wisdom decided to give the large Arsenal contingent our territory. Physically at times, some of the bigger Shrewsbury lads did try to regain some of that area. There were problems all afternoon but mostly between the Arsenal fans and the 'thin blue line'.

Just before the final whistle we went crazy as Peter Dolby scored with a header, so did the Arsenal fans as they tried to wreck lots of things. There was a fan on a floodlight.

I was glad I was in the Tech End. Alas my mum would not let me go to the replay!

Ron Morgan – Shrewsbury

I was a ten year old Salop fan who was on my way to watch a much anticipated League Cup replay against Blackburn Rovers, with the winner in line for Tottenham Hotspur. Not only that, but I had won a raffle to be ballboy – I couldn't wait.

Gay Meadow meanwhile was basking in everything which made it special. A game under floodlights, the swirling rain and an autumn wind which saw leaves falling off the surrounding trees. Whatever the result, you felt like you would remember the game anyway, it promised to be a great night.

And it was – Rovers snatching a winner in extra time. For me though I always wonder what role I played in that defeat. Eager to do my job well, almost to say 'thanks' to the raffle Gods that had got me in there, I made sure whenever the ball came near me, I picked it up and returned it to the team whose possession it was immediately, be it ourselves or the away side.

Only afterwards did I think, what if I had wasted a bit of time when Rovers were attacking? Surely no one would have expected a ten year old ball boy to be intentionally wasting time, it would have been an accident.

As it is Town still have never played Tottenham Hotspur in a competitive game, either home or away. But that also means the vast majority of Spurs fans have never visited Gay Meadow – and that, most definitely, is their loss.

Ant Thomas – Shrewsbury

To me, Gay Meadow was much more than just a football pitch. It was the place where I could spend time with my brother, just me and him amongst thousands of other fans, and share our passion for the club.

No girlfriends, no work, bills, or the myriad of other life problems – you didn't even have to answer your phone.

It was a safe place – a place where for ninety minutes I could escape from the world and just enjoy what was before me.

For that, I will always be thankful.

Peter Horton – Shrewsbury

I will never forget the old small dugouts which managers and substitutes would squeeze into.

Or the small office window to go and buy tickets or the old club shop to check out the latest choice of scarfs and hats.

The first occasion I was ball boy was for my 10th birthday when we played Bristol City. I was stationed in the corner of the Riverside and Station End. I was hopeful of seeing many corners taken in front of me, but instead there were very few, but included the one that Bristol City scored from to win 1-0!

Lewis Jones – Ipswich

It is time for a change now. It is sad, but the ground is basically worn out and knackered. Hopefully the new ground will be a more welcoming place for families, with facilities to make the diehard supporters proud.

Paul Yeomans – Shrewsbury

So how will I remember the old ground and what has motivated me to make a round trip of 200 miles for every home game for so many years?

Well, it certainly is not the amount of silverware or top international stars that grace the banks of the Severn. Nor is it the state of the art tin cladding that year after year seems to defy the elements and keep the Riverside intact. Nor indeed is it the five star luxury gents toilet that graces the Wakeman End, and which makes you wonder if you are in the 21st or 19th century.

Whilst Chelsea relay their pitch every weekend to ensure a bowling green finish, we wonder about the height of the Severn and whether the ploughed field that passes for our pitch will be fit for play.

There are few comparisons to Gay Meadow.

Hugh Dennis – Holmeswood, Lancashire

To many of us, Gay Meadow has been a reliable old friend, a constant, somewhere you can go to meet up with friends, socialise, have a laugh and a joke – but also somewhere you could get away from it all and lose yourself in football for two hours.

Nick Statham – Shrewsbury

My first experience of standing on the Gay Meadow terraces was during the 1993-1994 Championship winning season.

I had captured the bug of singing 'Come On You Blues' from the terraces.

It was a great experience to be part of the large vocal support as the Town won key matches against Chester City (3-0), Wycombe (1-0), Preston (1-0) and Northampton (2-1) to clinch promotion on April 23rd 1994.

Lewis Jones – Ipswich

Season 1983-84 saw attendances rise with 8,033 seeing the Shrews beat Sheffield Wednesday and 13,336 against Wolves. This was to be one of Shrewsbury's best seasons in the Football League.

As youngsters living on the west coast of Wales, we travelled twice monthly using the bonus of a Saturday saver ticket costing £1.80 return!

Arriving at the ground an hour early to see the Shrewsbury players arrive in their Austin Allegros etc. and to get an autograph or two, we would then take to our seats in the Wakeman Stand to eat a meat pie and read the programme while watching the players warm up and the regular characters roll in.

Happy days indeed.

Geraint Lewis James – Llandegfan, Anglesey

Before we lived in the centre of town, we used to come in by train. If we were late it was always more exciting seeing the fans already on the terraces from the grotty British Rail carriages that we were in, this added to the anticipation.

I used to like watching away fans clamber to the other side of the carriage to take a peek at Gay Meadow as our train passed. People who did not go to watch the football always assumed the rival fans would be fighting, but I probably had the best chats of my life with supporters wearing their club colours en route to Gay Meadow. We were a family, we supported football.

Karl Pickering – Shrewsbury

In the early days of league football, the PA system was quite good depending on which way the wind was blowing. I remember two announcements in particular when the game was ongoing. One asked the driver to return to his car because he had left the engine running. The other was because the driver's wife was locked in the car!

John Ryan – Aberdeen

I was a native of Meole Brace, Shrewsbury, and back in the 1950s the announcer's kiosk was at the back of the stand. The announcer was Brian Key. He used to play in a dance band that played at local venues like The Lion Hotel on Wyle Cop.

Brian received the half-time results via phone from an agency and I ran round with them to the half-time scoreboard. I climbed the ladder and handed them to the man in the box.

Great memories.

Philip Purslow – Worcester

I sincerely hope to be at the Grimsby match with my two grandsons for the last scheduled league match, but hopefully a further play-off match will take place.

How strange that the Wrexham match was the penultimate match, having been the first.

Wonderful memories, good times and bad times, but one hell of a proud Salopian.

Bob Edwards – Carterton

Of course what people wore changed through the sixties and seventies, as the general fashion changed in the country, the flat caps of the forties and fifties were disappearing. The sixties still had bobble hats and until the late sixties and early seventies, younger fans used to tie their scarf like a tie around their neck and also around a wrist too. People wearing jackets and ties had disappeared by the mid-sixties as casual wear was the order of the day. It must be said you still didn't see a lot of ladies at games back then.

Trilbys made a bit of an appearance, not just with older chaps but with the younger element in the early seventies, who had also started to favour smart blue three quarter length raincoats, and brogues with metal segs in the bottom so you knew they were coming. They also carried umbrellas but these were banned from grounds because they started to be used as weapons.

At one stage people stopped wearing scarfs and colours so they would not be targeted for violence by opposition fans. Beanies of course, emerged in the later decades giving a warm covering for the head, but without the naff looking bobble on top. All of it was a badge of sorts, no different to the Stone Island or Burb-

erry fashion statements of today.

Lads in the sixties and early seventies were starting to follow the trends into smarter wear. Skinheads morphed into suedeheads and then became bootboys. The suedes wore crombies and smart Levi Stayprest. Ben Sherman shirts were also popular. The bootboys obviously wore Dr Marten boots as their fashion accessories, with red socks and braces to keep their Levi Strauss jeans up.

I recall going to football matches up to about 1966 and not being aware of any organised or group violence. In fact people still used to wear rosettes on cup match days and people carried big rattles which very often were painted in the teams colours and could make a fair noise.

In the early seventies weapons started to be more evident, especially bottles and knives, and that's when the searches of people coming into grounds became commonplace. I remember a Reading fan being escorted out of the ground and he had a long piece of wood with nails in one end. How he had smuggled that in who knows?

All the above had the effect of deterring young fami-

lies and ladies from attending grounds, and I am sure also had some effect on the attendances. Something had to be done about it and stricter policing ensued.

Years passed, and by the time the eighties and nineties were here things had changed. Strict police enforcement and better control meant that any violence was generally avoided in the ground. Whilst I don't remember a date, the powers that be decided they were going to put all the away fans on the Station End and give us the rest of the ground. Obviously it was from here the Riverside became the singing fraternity's home, but it took a long while for us Station Enders to accept this as we felt we had been betrayed by the club.

However now trouble in grounds was rare, the families and ladies started to return.

There were other problems in the nineties and beyond especially at end of season games, when notably Middlesbrough and Derby ripped seats out of the stand and threw them like frisbees.

Streakers also played their part, all male as I recall, usually at televised big matches.

Ron Morgan – Shrewsbury

My biggest memory of the Gay Meadow does not come from a single game itself but rather over a period of time. I clearly remember when I first bought a car and one of the earliest trips that I took was back home to Shrewsbury and to the Meadow in particular.

Up to that point I had only been past the ground on the gyratory system, or on the English Bridge. That first trip to the car park is something that I will never forget.

The moment I stepped out of my car I felt at one with the area. I knew it was somewhere I belonged and as I walked around the outside I knew that my twenty years of support from afar had been leading up to this point – I'd only followed them on Ceefax and the fledgling internet mailing list.

The ground was closed but I knew I would be back. It took a few months for that return visit, as that first one was about June so there was no football on. Entering the ground for the first time in August, I took my seat in the Wakeman Stand. I can still remember which one it was, despite only sitting there a couple of times. The feeling I got at Gay Meadow was akin to the feeling I always got when I visited Stonehenge – it just felt right.

Dan Francis – Burton upon Trent

In the 93-94 season, when Town were champions, just the fact that every week, especially towards the end of the season, the Riverside was packed. When we scored, the celebrations were fantastic with everyone jumping around and dancing with people you hardly knew – but becoming friends with so many people just because of where you stood on the terraces. When we were confirmed champions, the chance to run onto the Gay Meadow pitch was so special. It was such a brilliant feeling that we had been promoted.

Penny Brown – Shrewsbury

Train crews would often park their steam engines on the embankment overlooking the Tech End.

When a match was on they would add to the cheering if the Town scored by blowing the engine's whistle.

John Ryan – Aberdeen

There is a song by one of my favourite bands, Faithless, called 'God is a DJ.' In it the words go, "This is my church, this is where I heal my hurt". Well that aptly sums up Gay Meadow for me.

There is a cliché that football is a religion, if this is true then my religion is Shrewsbury Town and Gay Meadow is my church and that is where I heal my hurt.

A defeat makes me sad, depressed and angry especially if the referee has been unjust to us or the other team has not deserved to win. And then the next fixture cannot come quick enough.

A win at the Meadow on a Saturday makes my weekend and my week.

It only became apparent to me in the latter stages of the last season, when I realised what a spiritual and special place Gay Meadow is to me.

I liken the floodlights to a church spire with the lights shining warmly upon the crowd, and the goal as an altar where we rejoice if the ball hits the back of the net - be it from a thirty yard screamer or a lucky header.

The fans who congregate sing their hymns of praise for the men in blue and amber.

The Town of Shrewsbury is very lucky to have so many church spires on its horizon, many of which can be seen from inside the ground.

Gay Meadow is my spiritual home and I will miss it so much.

John Andrews – Shrewsbury

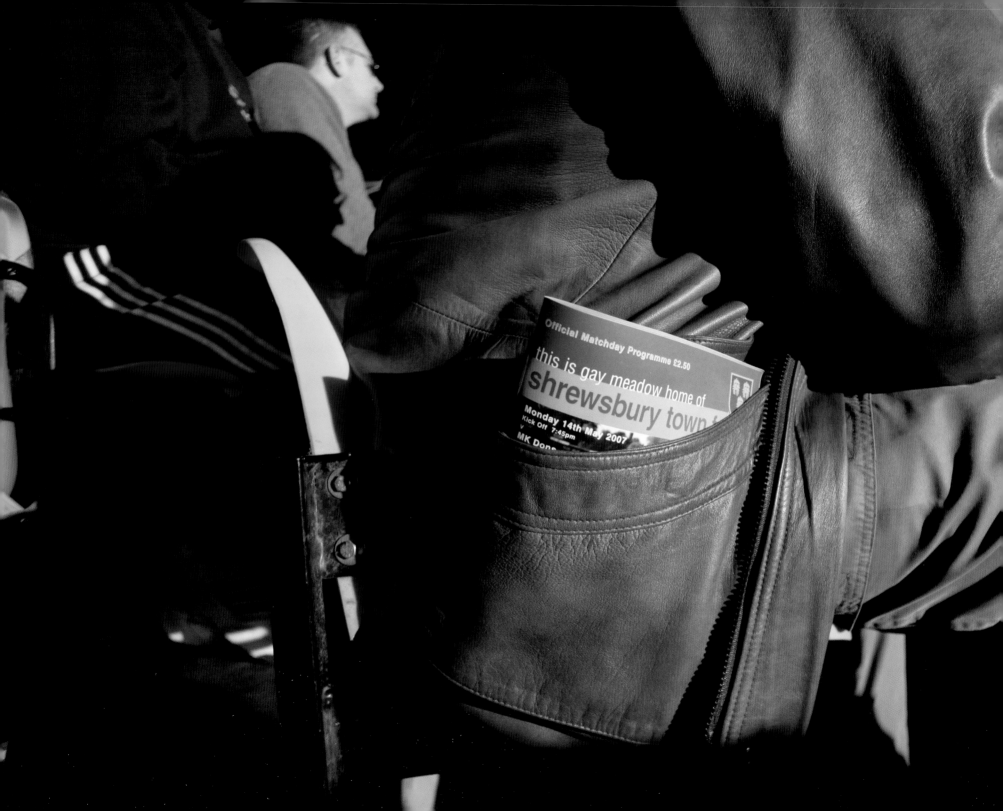

So it was Monday May 14th 2007 when Shrewsbury Town said farewell to Gay Meadow. It should have been the week before against Grimsby Town in Coca-Cola League Division Two, however after all the times the ground suffered at the hands of the elements resulting in a postponement, a perfect sunny Monday evening made my last day a happy one.

Chris Tooke – Shrewsbury

I am trying to compare the last game to a farewell tour by a favourite rock band or an inevitable funeral for a loved one who had been ill for a long time, but Gay Meadow deserves more than that in my heart. Whenever anyone I knew died, I would always seek refuge at Gay Meadow.

Seeing a young mother with a baby made me appreciate life when my father died. New blood into the world and all that.

Whatever I did, Gay Meadow was always there for me. There for me to hide in and be quiet, or there to be seen in and be shouting. Saying goodbye to loved ones, moving house and leaving behind happy memories were all easy to cope with as I always had Gay Meadow.

I probably sound like a very sad individual, but only now has it really struck home that we have to move on. But I'm not just saying goodbye to a place to just play football in. I will always be a Shrewsbury Town fan, but the Meadow was my spiritual home.

L.S. Williams – Shrewsbury

I am glad we had something to play for on that sunny Monday evening in May 2007 against MK Dons. When I left Gay Meadow for one last time I was focussed on going to Wembley for the Play-Off final.

If it had been a normal Shrewsbury Town season without success, I think there would have been more tears from grown men who have watched their team for years and years. It was indeed a sad day, however the football mattered that day and after all that is what we pay to go and watch.

Tony Giles – Hanwood, Shrewsbury

I treasured every moment of our last season at Gay Meadow. There is nowhere else like it on earth.

Willy Evans – Oswestry

In the old days I'd turn for a penny
at the end it was fourteen odd pound,
from Zimbabwe to Abergavenny
welcome legions of friends to our ground.
But now I stand quiet by the river
no more heard my familiar 'clunk' -
I just think to the future and quiver
"will I be thrown away with the junk?"
But then I was saved by a lady
to watch roses and daffodils grow,
in a garden so peaceful and shady
retirement's quite blissful you know!

Cuzz – Whitchurch

Even before I attended my first match I had always heard talk between my dad and grandads of 'going down the Mehdduh' – so it held sway over my imagination from quite a young age.

When I was taken to see the Town by my dad or grandad, we would watch the game from either the Centre or Wakeman stands and there was something about the place that I really connected with straight away. Perhaps I found a sense of identity in being a Shrewsbury fan and even a sense of belonging among the varied folk which made up the Meadow faithful.

Nick Statham – Shrewsbury

In 1979 when Paul Maguire used to take corner kicks, I always used to touch his back as he stood with his back to the crowd before putting his arm in the air, and then firing in the perfect corner. In the last few matches of 2007, my ten year old son Adam has tried to touch Neil Ashton before he has taken a corner kick.

I think in time when we look back on Gay Meadow, we will realise actually how lucky we were to be so close to the action.

Kevin Garbett – Hanwood, Shrewsbury

The final act of Gay Meadow is not a football game. It is not a terrace song. It is not a photograph, or a memory, or an event. It is the property deal that finances a new stadium and secures the future of our football club. Gay Meadow, our home, in its final act sacrifices itself for the sake of our future, a future we can all enjoy. New Meadow is not just a hope for our future, but it is a monument for all that has gone before.

David Matthias – Shrewsbury

As a resident of Nottingham, I am one of those so-called exiles supporting Shrewsbury Town. Where I am unusual is that I was an exile before I had even heard of the club. I was born in Oldham to a Latics-supporting father, so the odds of me ever stepping through the turnstiles at Gay Meadow were not high.

However, I had a Shropshire born mother and it is not surprising that my first football match was Shrewsbury v Oldham in 1965. I started cheering for Salop for no other reason than to annoy my dad. It was also a good start to my life as a fan, with Shrewsbury beating Oldham 3-1.

When I was a student I annoyed my house mates by refusing to go down the pub until I had heard the result of the final league match against Exeter in 1979. The BBC Nine O'Clock News actually went live to the ground at the final whistle and I watched the fans on the pitch celebrating the championship. I was both overjoyed at our success and sad that I was not there.

I will miss Gay Meadow, it has been a place of wildly varying emotions for me for more than forty years and saying goodbye to it will not be easy.

Steve Rogerson – Nottingham

Firstly I think it is important to say that I am not a Shrewsbury fan – or at least wasn't. Brought up following in my dad's footsteps, I am a Manchester United fan. My uncle was the black sheep of the family, a City fan who through his work had settled in Shrewsbury and regularly attended Gay Meadow for his Saturday fix of football. For many years when he saw me he would encourage me to come to a game, but for me it was not United and I resisted all attempts at persuasion.

Eventually on February 27th 1991, aged fourteen, I was worn down and attracted at the thought of seeing Arsenal in a classic potential FA Cup giant killing game. We all know it did not happen quite as we would like but I was gripped. Over the years I have continued attending games, the bug had definitely bitten. Whilst I am a season ticket holder at United, some of my fondest footballing memories have come from standing on the Riverside. I can honestly say so has my worst, the defeat to Carlisle confirming (thankfully temporary) exit from the Football League. The thing that has always kept me coming back are not only those moments that you share with so many others, but also the fact that when you bump into someone in a Shrewsbury shirt in far flung places, you know you've found a fellow sufferer, someone who has been through those things with you, sadly you can't always say that about United!

Matt Olley – Manchester

As a committed Town fan I made sure that when we were buying our first house at the end of 1991, it was to be within walking distance of the Meadow. At around the same time I became a car park steward, not the best job in the world as it meant that I would often miss the first few minutes of the match. The upside was free entry and a spare ticket for a mate.

The other drawback was the state of the car park. After a drop of rain it became a quagmire with puddles all over the place. I often had to select appropriate footwear, as ordinary shoes or trainers would leave you with soggy feet for the next few hours.

I guess the match against Hereford in 1993 was one of those games. After carrying out my pre-match duties I made my way into the ground. The match had already kicked off and just after I had passed in front of the Town dugout, Town scored a very early opener at the Wakeman End.

As Carl Griffiths peeled away in jubilation, he ran down the touchline towards me. Fortunately he was met by a couple of team mates, otherwise he might have ended up celebrating with a thirty something bloke in his yellow jacket (with STFC Steward emblazed on the back) and a lovely pair of green wellies!

Russ Teece – Shrewsbury

As a boy I remember the biggest of the big game days, there was always the problem of surviving the exit. Arms pinned to your side, shuffle your feet, stop, shuffle your feet and stop. Look up and see men everywhere and the sky above them.

When we got to the car we would wait for the cars in the main stream to let us out, someone shunts dad's car from behind, his foot slips off the clutch and we catapult into the main stream with horns blowing and skidding on the loose surface and off we'd go.

Malcolm Boswell – Greenville, South Carolina, USA

I would have been about nine or ten and my dad took me from Newtown. We were playing a team called Reading and parked behind the Station End and stood on the Station End. I remember we were losing 1-3 and my dad said we should try and get out of the ground with less than ten minutes to go. As we reached the car, a massive noise erupted and it was 2-3. Whilst we were wondering whether to go back in, another massive roar hit us and it was 3-3. From then on I used to go to every home game, spending all my pocket money on the bus from Newport where I used to board at school. Goodbye Gay Meadow, I will miss you and the times we have had.

Chris Richards – Shrewsbury

These days I watch the matches from the Riverside. My match day routine usually involves a pint or two and then onto the terraces, perhaps with an outrageously over priced cup of tea in one hand and a Yorkie in another.

Nick Statham – Shrewsbury

At fourteen I was selling programmes from a small hatch in the Tech End buffet. This was brilliant because you got to finish off any leftover sausage rolls. A year later I got promoted to the standing enclosure that is now the Family Stand. I still see the guys at the games that sold programmes at the same time, we are all of similar age.

My memories of those times are standing in a metal shack being shaken by a mob of Manchester City fans helping themselves to my programmes.

On retiring from programme selling, I stood on the Riverside before moving on to stand behind the Tech End goal, left post. Some of the characters there were amazing and I recall the smell of pies and alcohol wafting past.

Bob Martin – Shrewsbury

SHREWSBURY TOWN F.C.

THE CLUB HAS REQUESTED THAT

"ALL BOTTLE TOPS BE REMOVED AT POINT OF SALE"

My dad and grandad always went to Gay Meadow on match days, and as a youngster, I'd often wait for my dad to return, watching the results on TV as I did so. My first game was, as I recall, due to winning some tickets at Meole Brace Junior School, going with my dad to see Town play Derby. From then on I was bitten by the Town bug!

I remember visiting the changing rooms and meeting the players before a game in about 1984. We then sat right by the dugout to watch the game. I went to get my dad and me a couple of drinks, only to arrive back at my seat just as Gerry Nardiello scored. My dad's delight turned to my pain when he jumped up, knocking the hot drink I was carrying all over me. Thank goodness for the Town physio and his wet sponge!

Mark Hobden – Shrewsbury

I once played in the Staff v Supporters game. Getting changed in the dressing room, running the line, taking my bow as I went on for five minutes, being jeered from the sidelines (should not have invited my mother along to watch!) ... Ah it was perfection.

Goodbye old friend.

Dan Francis – Burton upon Trent

I got really annoyed when it was the school summer holidays and my family had to endure long drives to London where my parents tried to educate us on the sights of the capital. I was so bored when I was shown Buckingham Palace that I took to counting the black taxi cabs driving past to get rid of the boredom.

However, the following weekend it was the Shrewsbury Town open day. When Mike Thomas, the Commercial Manager, opened the dressing room door I saw where the team got changed. I then knew that being a Shrewsbury Town fan meant more to me than being a citizen cherishing the Queen and feeling proud of our historical monuments. Gay Meadow is a monument, an iconic place to my upbringing and life.

Trevor Jack – Shrewsbury

It all began in June 2003, the day we booked flights for a Christmas and New Year visit to family in Bridgnorth. The bitter disappointment of relegation out of the league was beginning to disappear and the optimism of a new start was beginning to grow. Even learning that Northwich Victoria were the team we would play didn't seem too bad.

I spent the fall listening to ShrewsWorld at home and at work. The wins away sounded good but the losses disappointing. The ShrewsWorld commentators do a fantastic job of not only describing the game, but also giving insights into the atmosphere and emotions of being a supporter. As September turned into October then November, the anticipation of Boxing Day and pushing through the turnstiles grew. Gay Meadow for all its faults and frailties is still a great place to watch football. Shrewsbury Town v Northwich Victoria was also to be my seven year old daughter's first Shrewsbury game. We were both excited!

Georgina and myself would watch the Columbus Crew a few times each summer. Watching soccer on balmy summer evenings, cheering a Crew win is appealing, but Boxing Day was the game we were looking forward to. Boxing Day was the day we would go to Gay Meadow.

December 26th finally arrived. I got my Spinal Tap shirt on and Father Christmas had conveniently delivered a Shrewsbury top for Georgina. We were set. We headed over to Shrewsbury for lunch in the Dun Cow with friends and family and then walked past the Abbey, past the Wakeman School to Gay Meadow. We paid our money, moved onto the Wakeman Terrace and stood and looked. "This is COOL!" she said. As much as we need the New Meadow, Gay Meadow is indeed cool. We stood in the drizzle for a few minutes and just soaked it all in.

We moved round to the Riverside and tried to keep dry. The atmosphere was good despite the weather and our expectations were high. My previous two games at the Meadow were two losses with a combined score of 2-9. "We should beat the Vics," I kept saying, "we should beat the Vics."

The rain kept pouring and as the first half progressed, a little frustration started to creep in. Lots of chances, but none put away. Just before half-time the first goal went in. Dad and daughter cheered and I realised that I felt prouder that we were there, together, rather than the fact that we had just taken the lead.

In that moment, my Ohio born daughter was as much a proud Salopian as me. Whether by osmosis or indoctrination, she is a Shrewsbury Town supporter. A couple more goals, a couple more hugs and a solid win. Gay Meadow that afternoon, for this exile, was indeed a cool place to be.

Georgina's first and as it turns out last visit to the Meadow was summed up as she told grandad that standing at Shrewsbury Town was much better than sitting at the Columbus Crew.

Richard Cole – Cleveland, Ohio, USA

In 1950, standing opposite the grandstand where to my mind the rich people sat, when 10/- (ten shillings) was a fortune, I always thought it odd they paid more to be blinded by the sun, which of course shines onto the seats.

Bob Edwards – Carterton

How fitting it was that the sun should shine so bright over good old Gay Meadow for the last home game. How I have sat in the stand and cursed the sun, having to watch matches over the years either with one eye closed, or with a hand obscuring my view.

Yet on that last day it was the memories that watered my eyes, not the sun.

Roger Groves – Shrewsbury

7,126 of us in Gay Meadow heard referee Mr K Stroud blow his whistle for the last time on Monday May 14th 2007. I wanted him to be near me when the final act took place as I stood in my normal spot on the Wakeman End, with Laura's Tower overlooking us in between the floodlights on this final night.

However rather annoyingly he ended the game in the opposite half signalling towards the tunnel.

Like a judge sentencing someone to life, or a doctor proclaiming someone was dead, Mr Stroud declared the last rites over our ground. From this point on there would be no more.

Although the game was good and we were still in the hunt for the play-offs, I went into another world. I half expected ghosts from the past to emerge from the floodlights wearing blue and white, and blue and amber football kits.

So this was the end I thought. I didn't know if I should cheer the lads off the pitch after watching ninety minutes of football. Did it actually matter?

What really mattered was that after a season full of postponements and in true Shrewsbury Town fashion, the last scheduled game against Grimsby was not the last. THIS was now the end of Gay Meadow.

I am glad the football on display mattered that night and Shrewsbury Town had something to aim for, otherwise going to the Meadow would have been like visiting a poorly relative and waiting for their last breath. With the funeral march leaving the ground, walking over the bridge and back to our drinking dens in Town trying to get a peak of the floodlights being switched off for the last time.

However because of the television, I assumed they must have been packing up their equipment as the lights seemed to be on all night.

Thanks to Gary Peters and the team, the excitement of the play-offs stopped a lot of emotion. It is only now that tears fill my eyes as I remember everything before me.

Peter Harris – Shrewsbury

As the referee ended the last game, I could not picture people living on the land where our ground sits. I trust that my memories will overpower the reality of what will be. I will always have pictures and footage to fall back on. How fitting that the MK Dons match was broadcast live to the nation. That did not happen at Fellows Park, the old ground of Walsall, or Sealand Road at Chester City. I feel smug and am proud of that.

Oscar Cousins – Shrewsbury

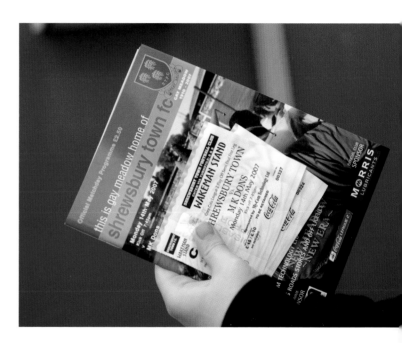

The atmosphere on that last night was very, very special. I was so glad JUST to have been able to get tickets and be there, even though not in my normal place. For me, the fact that it was a night match made it extra special. The most touching, poignant moment was seeing the floodlights come on. Those floodlights, towering above the trees, form an iconic image.

If I had been there long enough to see the floodlights go out, and darkness descend, then maybe I would have become a bit emotional.

Pauline Griffiths – Wigan

: 2007

: 2007

Line A

Line B

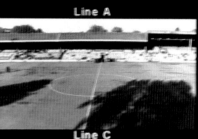

18:31:59

Line C

Line D

Quadspli

TX HD

: 2007

cam 21/ 1

cam 21/ 2

SONY

POWER

I have thought long and hard about my favourite memory of the Gay Meadow. Games that excited me, cup exploits, the great disappointment of relegation, great players, friends I have made through my support of the club over the last 26 years. However, my abiding memory will not be of players, supporters or games I have witnessed. No, for me, it is simple. I will miss standing on the terraces to watch my favourite football team.

As an over fifty year old, I was brought up on football played at ancient stadiums, breezy, freezing days with a cup of hot Bovril to stave off the creeping damp and cold getting beneath my coat. I have supported teams wherever I have lived and have always sought to stand to watch a game.

There is something more dynamic, more intimate about standing to watch a game. To leap with joy with those around you when Town score a goal. To watch Bizzy run down the sparsely populated Riverside terrace, deliriously inebriated, waving his scarf in triumph!

The communal frustrations at a poor performance. The mingling of friends and acquaintances swapping views and stories of other games. The exhilaration of being in a packed standing area as it sways and pulses with the turning points of the game, will stay with me forever.

So my abiding memory of the 'old girl' will be an experience that will no longer be available to me. Standing to watch a game is a truly symbiotic relationship between me and the ground.

Martin James – Shrewsbury

I always treasure my visits to the Meadow but this last season the poignancy has been enormous.

I found myself thinking, which would be the last night game? The last penalty? The last victory? The last goal at the Wakeman End? – Kelvin Langmead v Grimsby Town and so forth.

The Grimsby game had so much riding on it and then finally the realisation that there was to be one final last hurrah.

Paul Gladwell – Edinburgh

I am trying to persuade my husband that we need to go, but he is saying that we have had an expensive month. True, but play-offs don't happen every season. It is worth going into the overdraft for!

Pauline Griffihts – Wigan

As I only lived in Abbey Foregate, I used to go down to watch the last fifteen minutes of most home games, as they opened the big gate to let early leavers out. Pocket money did not stretch to gate money back then.

Tony Wellings – Preston

Older fans will remember the early 1970s when miners' strikes led to power cuts meaning clubs could not use floodlights for evening games. Consequently in spring, Town played a number of mid-week games with a 4.30pm kick-off. The only way I could get to the match against Cardiff in the Welsh Cup was to go straight to the Meadow from playing hockey at school, without going home first. As a result I took my hockey stick into the ground and carried it with me throughout the match!

I cannot imagine being let into the ground these days with such an offensive weapon.

Richard Hobbs – Nottingham

As a sixteen year old, I quit my Saturday job at Woolworths as they would not give me the afternoon off to go to the Liverpool FA Cup match. I woke up on the day of the match and turned the radio on to hear that the game had been postponed due to snow. I was still pleased that I had made my point to the assistant store manager about the importance of Shrewsbury Town Football Club.

Paul Davies – Welwyn Garden City, Herts

One of my first memories of Gay Meadow was when I travelled up to Shrewsbury from Windsor with some Watford fans en route to the FA Cup game in 1991. Not being from Shrewsbury, my alliance was from my dad's side. I saw some strange looking device/building/board in the corner of the ground with lots of letters on it. Realising it was some old fashioned scoreboard, I had to look at my programme in order to work out what the half-time scores were.

Chris Miro – Windsor

One Saturday morning in November 1956, my brothers and I searched high and low for wooden cotton reels from my mother's sewing box. Then we went to aunts, cousins and neighbours for more. When dad deemed we had enough, it was off to Gay Meadow, just me and him as no one else wanted to go. The cotton reels were to insulate a telephone cable from the Directors Box to the old scoreboard. Dad spent all morning up the stepladder banging nails through the centre of the reels into the top of the wall so the cable could be strung.

Len Crane – Shrewsbury

As a youngster I got a great thrill from spotting the men running up the scoreboard ladder at Gay Meadow. They then delivered the scores to the other men inside before they were displayed for all to see.

It was as if I was not supposed to notice them and felt great joy that I had seen the mechanics of this great system in place.

I was not very good at football and as my school friends wanted to be Paul Maguire, I wanted to be the man who worked inside the scoreboard.

Jeremy Hall – Stoke-on-Trent

When I was a child, the joys at half-time were clutching the programme in one hand, and reading the A-X fixtures on the scoreboard to see what was happening up and down the country.

I also had the joy at being at the Marine match (11-2) when double figures were used not for the goal scorer but for the number of goals scored. It is one Gay Meadow fixture which is sadly missed

Stephen Hutchison – Admaston

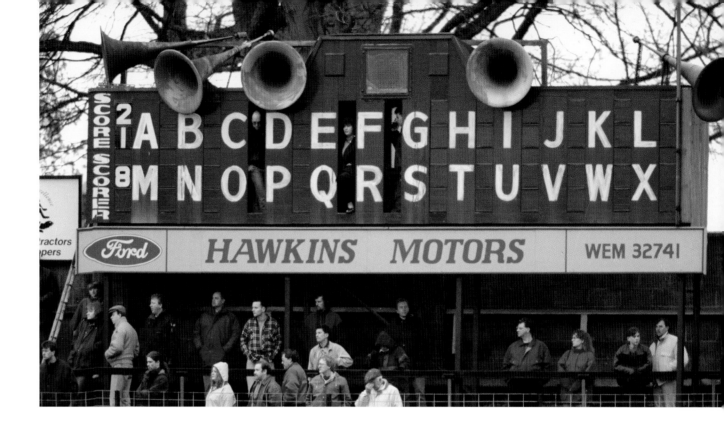

As a travelling supporter I found Gay Meadow unique in many ways. In my youth when I was following West Ham it was unfashionable to actually like the away ground you were visiting as Upton Park was home.

Saying that, I always had a soft spot for Shrewsbury and especially the scoreboard. It reminded me of one of those mobile PA caravans that schools used for sports day.

Even though the loudspeakers were huge, when I was in the away end I could never hear what was being said.

Looking back, one of my favourite lifetime memories of following West Ham United was peering over to look at the programme/newspaper that Shrewsbury would produce, memorising the fixtures, like N = Sheffield Wednesday v Newcastle for example. Feeling my presence, this guy would look over his shoulder and stare at me but I would quickly look forward to the scoreboard and try to memorise the half-time results corresponding them to the letters in front of me.

I remember having a huge argument on the way home as I had told my friend that Charlton were losing 0-2 at half-time but on the radio we heard that they had won 1-0.

J. White – London

In his definitive book on 'The Football Grounds of Great Britain' author Simon Inglis described it thus..."On the far side of the (Wakeman) terrace is a lovely old half-time scoreboard built in 1936 and adorned with a disproportionately large loudspeaker."

Well, in fact he was not quite right. In its heyday, to my knowledge, the scoreboard boasted five loudspeakers – old gramophone style speakers – which I agree were disproportionately large compared to the wooden blue rectangle structure on which they were positioned.

I for one will always bemoan the loss of the wonderful old scoreboard which I always considered to be a quintessential feature of Gay Meadow. In fact I felt that the Meadow never had quite the same character following the demolition of it in May 1996.

My dad used to stand on the Wakeman Terrace with me positioned on a stool at the perimeter wall. Some of my first recollections as an impressionable six year old boy at Gay Meadow in 1966 revolved around that grand old scoreboard. On rainy days my father used to make his way to the rear of the terrace and this was my chance to scamper underneath the board seeking the only available shelter from the rain. Incidentally, another clear memory from those days was the sound of a man blowing a hunting horn each time Town attacked the Wakeman End.

But the scoreboard itself was always a hive of activity. It was a wonder to behold the scurry of men and boys up and down ladders and out of shutters, arranging the white numbers against letters A-X that corresponded with a key to the day's fixtures, as printed in the match programme. It was as if by magic that the half-time scores up and down the country were conveyed to eagle eyes, the anticipation of watching the scores materialise was far better than today's instant radio.

But the scoreboard was more than just that. It regularly blasted out the latest tunes of the day. I well remember the smell, sound and feel of the Meadow on days and nights when anthems of the day rang out.

I loved the shape and sound of the old scoreboard. I suppose like a lot of things in life which are good, they come to an end at sometime, and for me the demise of the scoreboard took on an almost spiritual dimension.

It was May 4th 1996, the last day of the disappointing 1995/96 campaign. Town had struggled but ended safe in Division Two. On this day, a sunny mild one, Town were to play their final fixture at Turf Moor against Burnley. In truth the fixture was meaningless.

However unbeknown to me something was stirring at The Meadow. I felt a strange and irrational compul-

sion to go down to the ground on that Saturday morning. Men in coats armed with heavy tools were systematically demolishing the old scoreboard. It was terrible to see them tearing away sixty years of history and while I was there I could see the old wooden structure being torn to pieces.

I asked them why they were doing it and they said it was to create room for an access entrance from the Wakeman School gardens to the back of the ground, incidentally a scheme which failed to materialise!

I felt very sad at what happened. I just could not believe that the old scoreboard was to be no more. I had heard nothing about the proposal to demolish it and in view of subsequent events, I still wonder why it was done. The only saving grace for me was that I managed to salvage a single piece of the broken wood which bore the letter 'S'.

To this day I proudly display this symbolic relic in 'the Shrewsbury suite' at my house in Ipswich.

This is a tangible reminder to me of what was once a marvellous and functional structure. Sadly we will never see its like again as times have moved on with the electronic age, but for me the memories abide and no-one can expunge those.

Mike Schorah – Ipswich

It was a cold January afternoon, FA Cup fourth round 1981. Ipswich Town were visiting with a team of all-stars. My brother, my dad and I arrived at the ground at 2.00pm and entered the enclosure. (The bottom tier of what was converted to the away seating).

We stood in the usual spot with my brother and I leaning over the wall, dad stood behind. By ten to three the enclosure was full to capacity, what was usually a pleasant experience was getting a bit uncomfortable with the amount of people crammed in. With 18,000 in the Meadow it was rocking.

An observant steward spotted the distress and came over to see if he could help and played a blinder, carrying my brother and I over the wall and sitting us in a first aid dugout in the corner virtually on the touchline.

By 3 o'clock every child in the enclosure was lined up on the side of the pitch to watch the game. I still remember Colin Griffin nudging Paul Mariner over the touch-line and into the row of kids who were now sitting in front of the advertising boards.

We drew 0-0 and lost the replay.

Dave Armitage – Shrewsbury

I remember when the chairman told the internet people to give less emphasis to the Gay Meadow toilets when they did some pages on our fine ground. The ladies were always acceptable in my mind but I was intrigued to know what the fuss was about.

At the last match against Grimsby Town when everyone had nearly left, I knew this was my last chance to see what the fuss was all about. Firmly holding my breath, I had a peek into the Riverside gents!

All I can say is that I'm fully behind the chairman and hope the facilities for the lads are better in the new stadium!

Tracy Evans – Oswestry

We were playing Everton in 1961, Gay Meadow was full to overload, or it seemed so at the time. Half-time came and my pre-match drinking had got the better of me. The queue to the gents was agonisingly long so I ran into the ladies.

That night Peter Dolby helped Town to a famous victory and I don't think I have ever been happier, however I also experienced the fear that someone would see me exiting the ladies lavs.

My grandson has so much cheek and has no fear that I envy the youth of today. He would probably enter into the ladies even with ladies in there if he were in such a similar position. For me though as a child of the 30s, I still feel shameful of my actions to this day!

W. Reed – Shifnal

Without being perverse, I always wondered what it was like in the ladies at Gay Meadow.

Greg Harris – Shrewsbury

I absolutely hate wearing my suit for work. I look up at the Wakeman School and think of when I had to wear that horrible uniform. But when it is the weekend, I put on my Town shirt and go to my second home, Gay Meadow. There is a saying, 'most business is done on the golf course', but I have made many an important decision drinking a half-time cup of tea on the terraces with my business colleagues.

Tony McDonald – Telford

Born in Shrewsbury in 1939, my first visit to the Meadow was at the start of the 1946/47 season. It was either a reserve match against Boldmore St. Michael or Brierley Hill in the Birmingham League, who for a seven year old were two big teams near Birmingham! In those early days my father and I stood behind the goal at the Station End behind the wall. Midland League matches were also watched from there. In 1949 we switched to the Tech End, as it was called then.

One memorable occasion was getting ex-England international Eddie Hapgood's autograph on his final match when playing for Town at left back in the 1948/49 season, jumping over the wall with many others during the pre-match kick in.

We lived by the river at Coton Hill up to 1948 and walked to the ground via Castle Gates, past the Infirmary, down St. Mary's Street and Wyle Cop. The match attendance could always be estimated by the number of pedestrians in those pre-car days. Moving to Copthorne and Harlescott in 1950, we travelled in by the S13 and S9/10/11 buses to Barker Street, and walked to the Meadow using different routes via Princess Street, Milk Street or the passages to Town Walls. Visitors by train often used the short cut from the platform to the Gay Meadow car park under transport police supervision.

For the first Football League match against Wrexham on Monday August 21st 1950, we squeezed into the right of the goal at the Tech End, but such was the squash, the first crowd control at the Meadow saw us moved into the reserve side terrace by the wall under the press box, opposite the six yard line. After the excitement of this first game, we adopted a position on the Riverside terrace, firstly by the wall and then at the back fence opposite the 18 yard line. With no away supporters segregation in those days, visitors were spread around the ground, with occasionally a mass behind the goal at the Tech End. Surprisingly there were never any problems and chants of later years were very few. Oldham supporters were the first to use the '2-4-6-8' chant when massed behind the Tech End goal.

As the years progressed, I, with my fellow teenagers, stood under the Riverside and saw the great Arthur Rowley from this position. Special buses to Harlescott after the match started in Abbey Foregate, opposite the Abbey Church. Big attendances were common with toilet use always a problem, buffet facilities were limited and as half-time breaks were only ten minutes then, there was no time to wander too far.

Reserve team matches in the Football Combination were good, as teams like Arsenal and Spurs would often play first team players. Gay Meadow saw an amateur international in the late forties and the Town played Dundalk from Eire in 1949 and lost, which was a bit of a culture shock for a ten year old, who thought all English teams were invincible!

Marching bands were common in the 1950s, military and civilian, and if my memory serves me right, the Dagenham Girl Pipers (a big hit then) also gave a pre-match display. Also The Town came on to the pitch to the tune of the 'Liberty Bell'.

Bob Edwards – Carterton

In the late 1950s I sold programmes and because of this, I received a free pass. With a mate we sold them off a trestle table just below the old wooden press box which was then sited on the open terrace, now the Wakeman Stand.

After selling the programmes we were allowed to find a seat at the back of what is now the Centre Stand.

Philip Purslow – Fernhill Heath, Worcester

I had just turned ten when I went with my cousin, Miss Irene Haynes, now Mrs Owen, to the Gay Meadow for the first match in the Football League, (3rd Div North) against Wrexham.

The date was Bank Holiday Monday 21st August 1950. We stood behind the goal at the Station End, which would become the place where we stood to watch the Town over the years until the terrace was allocated to visiting fans.

On that memorable day, the Town beat Wrexham 2-1, and I recall running onto the pitch at the end of the game, and patting the players on the back as they went up the tunnel to celebrate their first league win. We had problems getting into the match, due to the large crowd, as did many others, which led to the management having to purchase new and better turnstiles.

The Town's colours were blue and white on that day. How things have changed, rosettes and wooden rattles were the norm in those days, and not the coloured hats and shirts that adorn the Meadow today.

As I looked forward to the final league match against Grimsby, I took my place in the same spot where it all began 57 years ago in the Station End. How many supporters who were at the Grimsby Town game were also there for the first ever league match against Wrexham?

W. Mike Jones – Shrewsbury

When I was at college in Cornwall and being a student with no money, I hitch-hiked home for a home game on a freezing cold Friday night in 1977. It took me ages. I got stuck at Bristol Gordano services and I thought I would sleep the night there as it was too cold to stand out and hitchhike. I hoped for a good lift in the morning.

So I rang home first to let my folks know, only to find out that they had called the game off due to a frozen pitch. What a nightmare! So I hitchhiked back to Cornwall on the Saturday – the things you do to see the Town play!

Ron Morgan – Shrewsbury

I have attended matches at Gay Meadow ever since 1958 and during my student days had to hitchhike to the games from Craven Arms. This led to many inter-esting journeys to and from my beloved Gay Meadow and many long walks in between Shrewsbury and Craven Arms.

In one particular incident a lorry driver from Shrewsbury gave me a lift at about midday for a usual 3pm kick-off. We got to Shrewsbury early so he offered to take me for a pint of beer in the Hole in The Wall. Although only 17 and fairly new to drinking I readily agreed. Several pints later I made my way to the match only to spend the entire match feeling ill and sitting throughout the game on the Station End steps.

Hitching home was always problem-atic. I was once marooned on Church Stretton bypass in driving rain and sleet at about midnight and walked the last eight miles home, drenched to the bone.

Colin James – Wistanstow

I started my Shrewsbury Town experience in the Family Stand. A 3-2 defeat by Leeds United in December 1982, aged four, was the moment I knew it hurt to lose. In time our family moved into the Wakeman Stand for some lean years in football terms, until I finally flew the nest of family outings and stood with my mates on the Wakeman End in time for our 1994 Championship. Going to university saw another step up, this time to the Riverside with singing and friendships and a sense of belonging.

David Matthias – Shrewsbury

In February 1988 I sat in the Wakeman Stand with my dad and saw the Town win 2-1 with a goal each from Bernard McNally and Victor Kasule against Swindon Town. From those early moments, there was only one place to go, and that was to Gay Meadow.

I loved the unique setting of Gay Meadow. The walk down Wyle Cop, over the English Bridge and along the entrance road to the ground added to the character of going to the match.

As I began to become a regular in the Family Enclosure, there would be great friendly banter between the young Shrewsbury supporters and the visiting fans that sat in the Station End of the main stand.

Lewis Jones – Ipswich

My first memory of visiting the Gay Meadow was the League Cup game against Everton in 1961. I was ten years of age and my grandfather took me. I remember sitting on wooden benches in the C Stand (now the stand where the away supporters sit). I then became a very active Town supporter, both home and away. I always stood on the Station End, getting there early enough to be able to lean or sit on the wall. It used to cost me 1/6d to gain entry. I remember Eric Brodie scoring in the Station End goal and celebrating with the fans.

We have watched the Town from the Centre Stand for the last few years and will be very sorry to say goodbye to the Meadow.

Hilary Jones – Shrewsbury

One of my earliest memories of the Gay Meadow was the commemorative game the Town played against West Ham United after the 1966 World Cup Final. Because the England team had trained at Lilleshall and West Ham provided three key players, they visited Shrewsbury for a friendly match to raise funds for Lilleshall.

Bobby Moore captained the visitors, majestic in defence as ever, with Martin Peters also in defence. The only disappointment was Geoff Hurst not making an appearance, although as Meat Loaf would say, "two out of three ain't bad".

In those days the main stand had terracing in front alongside the pitch, and I remember a very young Harry Redknapp running over with a bouquet of flowers to give to a woman standing next to me in the crowd.

Mark Martin – Orpington, Kent

When we got relegated to the Conference I was at the game with my son Alex who was ten at the time. He was crying so much I had to give him a big hug and we ended up being on Midlands Today News. We even got into The Sun newspaper. I remember telling him that it would be for one year only and I wasn't sure how true it was!

Jayne Dovaston – Ellesmere

There were always many good vantage points from the Wakeman classrooms and I remember a particular favourite was a room on the C floor, which allowed us to watch reserve games on Wednesday afternoons. To pass the time at lunchtime, we had a competition as to who could throw a paper aeroplane the furthest down the Gay Meadow pitch. I remember one of my friends managing to get his plane, albeit with the help of a strong gust of wind, from the Wakeman to the Station End, a great achievement. I also remember the look on the groundsman's face when he saw the pitch a few hours later, there must have been thirty paper aeroplanes strewn across the pitch, he didn't look too impressed and actually I think he complained to the school about us.

I used to see a lot of players around the Meadow on the way to the playing fields or after school. I recall seeing Nigel Jemson and speaking to him sometimes, he was always a very friendly guy.

Andy Ward – Shrewsbury

Crystal Palace at home in 1974, we lost 2-4, but I remember my first game at Gay Meadow for two reasons. There were two streakers, and it featured on the Big Match on television the next day with Hugh Johns commentating.

Richard Owen Roberts – Tywyn, Gwynedd

We haven't had TV cameras visit us much at the Meadow, but when we have it has been one hell of a game! Palace '74, Man City '79, the Ipswich epics in the eighties and of course Everton. However since the nineties I think there was always a TV camera in the stand, which thankfully recorded that game when we beat Marine 11-2, capturing all eleven goals.

Richard Hughes – Shrewsbury

I remember sitting on a deserted terrace in bright sunshine with Dave Howell on a warm August afternoon in 1978.

The terraces were sparsely populated for that match. I sat with him again in evening sunshine for the last game of the season against Exeter City ten months later, with a full house and the noise of the crowd ringing in my ears.

Vince Jones – Martinstown, Dorchester

I was born in Shrewsbury and started supporting the Town when my dad took me in 1957. I was nine. They used to run 'football special' buses from Harlescott. I moved away in 1969 but am still a fervent supporter. I remember vividly the state of the pitch during the winter months. There wasn't a blade of grass to be seen apart from around the corner flags!

The whole pitch was a sea of mud which made for some very interesting encounters. The ball never bounced during the whole match.

John Ryan – Aberdeen

I followed Town home and away in the old Second Division. I was fond of Ipswich and Watford as they had revolutionary electronic scoreboards and had sprite characters jumping up and down when a goal went in. I used to be ashamed of the set up down the Meadow, but as time moved on, a hand written message to supporters taped on a window suited the old girl rather than a mass of electronic lights flickering away showing information. Gay Meadow surpassed the time when it became embarrassing to the point it was unique and unlike the other stadiums in the land.

John Staples – Birmingham

It wasn't just the football that captured my imagination but all the match day sights, sounds and smells. The wafts of cigarette smoke (although I never became a smoker), the coarse but amusing language, standing up to celebrate whenever Town scored a goal, chanting 'OFF OFF OFF' whenever an opposing player committed a particularly heinous foul and slowly shuffling down the Narrows after the game with talk (usually disgruntled talk) of the game everyone had just witnessed filling the air, to name a few of the experiences I came to know and love.

Nick Statham – Shrewsbury

When I used to sit in the old wooden Centre Stand, there was an old man who used to smoke a pipe throughout the game. It stank. I hated it.

These days of course we are not allowed to smoke in the stands, but I was in a bar in Ireland sometime ago and this smell wafted towards my nose. My initial reaction was to waft the smoke away, but all of a sudden it reminded me of Gay Meadow and the tobacco that man used to smoke.

Sitting in Dublin, my mind took me back to Sammy Irvine, Ian Atkins and Paul Maguire with me and the people around me stamping our feet whenever we had a corner.

I am actually an anti-smoker, but that smell brought back so many memories.

Gary Sellers – Shrewsbury

What I will remember most about Gay Meadow is the sense of community. I have made so many good friends over the years on the Riverside who have changed my life so much.

I love terracing and the interaction with other supporters that the terracing gave me. Many people I have got to know personally through standing here and there, and countless others I can stand and talk to for ninety minutes, and I still don't even know their names!

We celebrated together and commiserated together.

So thank you Gay Meadow for all the wonderful friends I have made and the impact the old place has had in my life.

It has changed me forever.

Peter Maddox – Shrewsbury

Early memories were sitting in the old wooden grandstand with my late grandfather.

I lost a shoe in the post match pitch invasion following the famous defeat of Manchester City in the FA Cup in 1979. The shoe was found after the terraces had emptied. I have stood on the Riverside ever since and will miss the banter of the terraces.

Neil Wootton – Shifnal

My dad held up tickets to the French window as me and my brother Kevin were playing in the deep snow outside, but I was only really interested in finishing building a snowman.

I was just about tall enough to look over the concrete wall complete with my Parka jacket and first ever blue and amber scarf.

Who knows if I would have been a life long fan if I had not been to this first match.

Gary Bright – Shrewsbury

On the morning of the match I got up with the feeling I used to get every Saturday when Salop were at home – excitement and anticipation.

That day there was so much snow, I was wondering if the game would be on.

Football Focus did a feature on Grand-stand, that added to the anticipation.

Then I set off for the ground wondering if the game would be called off.

There was a buzz of excitement at the ground, going through the turnstiles and looking at the pitch. I remember thinking what a brilliant job people had done to clear all the snow, which was piled up round the touchline.

I asked my mum to record the commentary, which meant sticking a portable tape recorder in front of the radio. I had the whole of the second-half on tape and listened to it many times after. I also recorded the Wolves replay in a similar way, unfortunately they are both long gone.

David Hawksworth – West Yorkshire

In most football grounds home supporters were given the luxury of covered accommodation, while any area of open terracing was allocated to the opposition. Gay Meadow though had to be different. Once segregation came in the visitors had the use of the partially covered Station End, while home supporters got the open terrace, the Wakeman End.

Jim Simpson – Shrewsbury

Anyone that chose to make the Wakeman End his, or possibly her, vantage point did so in defiance of logic. While the sun might gently caress those standing on the concrete terraces in April or August, most of the football season occupied a far more uncertain climate of wind and rain. A burst of rain might cause a scramble to seek sanctuary under the scoreboard, but one summer even that small refuge disappeared. The steps of the terracing remained relatively shallow and the shorter individuals would find their view of the action slightly obscured; for those people a small spot on the ledge halfway up the back wall was a prized acquisition. In the dark days of perimeter fencing many found that the view of the action was dissected by the squares of a heavy mesh. As for toilet facilities it is enough to say that the installation of a corrugated roof seemed like a move into the world of five star hotel treatment.

Yet for reasons of bizarre taste, convenience or necessity the Wakeman End was the guarded territory of some dedicated football supporters. Indeed, for a short time the Riverside was restricted strictly to 'members only'. It only needed one of a group of mates to leave his members card on the kitchen table – or for someone to refuse to register with the membership scheme – the Wakeman End was the only available part of the ground. By default it became home.

When the rain lashed down the fainter hearted might discretely move round the corner to seek the protection of the Riverside cover.

However, the fanatical Wakeman Ender would firmly stand his ground not budging an inch, like a soldier determined to defend regimental honour even after the firing of the last round of ammunition. This resolution would come at a cost though – water would

soak towards the skin, woolly hats would be ruined and wet clothes would have to be hung up immediately on returning home.

The Wakeman End was commonly regarded as the province of the moody moaner, quick to criticise and to voice displeasure. There again, if someone had frequently stood in the open and got doused on regular occasions, and the cold and the rain had chilled the bones and got into the joints, perhaps a curmudgeonly outlook on the football was understandable. However, whatever the discomfort suffered by the Wakeman Ender it all paled with the thrill of trying to suck the ball into the net, or the outright unrestrained joy of a late winner being scored right in front of you and as the players celebrated with you that sweet feeling you were a part of it all.

Ian Jones – Shrewsbury

The tension as Salop led Everton 2-1 was incredible, the trouble was I was sat about 1,000 miles away in an Army camp in Kosovo.

The final whistle went and I remember jumping around like a lunatic. An impromptu party followed whereby everyone in the bar was promoted to the rank of Shrewsbury Town fan Class Three for the night.

The next few days passed in a blur, suddenly it was time for the cup draw for the next round. Listening attentively, I again let out a whoop when the name of Chelsea appeared directly after ours. Then to bring me down to earth one of the young soldiers said, "Shame you can't make it Sir".

By God, I was not going to miss this one, but looking at my options, it didn't look good. One thousand miles away, no season ticket, Priority or Super Blues card and no leave left.

Plan A – Phone the club up. "You're phoning from where?" and "sorry no chance" about sums up that option.

Plan B – Approach the Colonel. "Yes RSM Parton, if you can get the Battalion some positive PR you can go." Feeling slightly happier I managed to blag tickets on an Italian Army flight landing in Serbia before transferring by plane back to the UK.

Now the small problem of tickets. Salop being Salop came through and because of the generosity of one member of staff, I got a family pack. So leaving Kosovo, I proceeded via Serbia and an RAF Hercules which was, of course, late. We eventually landed in Oxfordshire and the duty driver whisked me down to London. I quickly grabbed the family and we were soon Salop bound.

Arriving in Shrewsbury about three hours before kick-off saw us joining a long queue on a bitterly cold night. The game itself remains a blur, to be honest I left dead on ninety minutes to make a quick getaway. We arrived home in London gone midnight. I was back on a plane by 0730hrs and was back in Kosovo before lunch.

I was knackered, skint and in trouble with the Colonel but was it worth it? You bet it was!

Stu Parton – Windsor

It was a strange feeling really, I had rehearsed it a thousand times in my mind, like a speech or a presentation you should always be prepared to have something to fall back on.

The game was played at a fast pace, no time to think of it being the last match, both teams having a go, both unable to strike a hammer blow.

As the final whistle blew I jumped up with joy and relief, we were still well and truly in with a chance of Wembley and promotion, then all of a sudden my thoughts changed to sadness, no more Gay Meadow. No more the little rituals we all have, how things must change, there is no choice.

I remember looking around seeing the different expressions on people's faces, some like me just standing, the heart beating a little faster, that sickening feeling of wanting to cry and laugh at the same time.

I stood for a while to try to savour the moment, wrestling with how I wanted to remember the very last moment. I looked for my son on the Riverside, one last look at the clock, a quick look up to the floodlights, a wave to a mate I'd just spotted, I moved along to by the Family Stand, children were crying. Some people were on the pitch.... it was all over.

Goodbye Gay Meadow.

Roger Groves – Shrewsbury

The game against Milton Keynes Dons, whilst loaded with significance for football reasons, was still difficult to take in.

I ensured I HAD to get my usual spot by arriving well before the gates opened.

As for the penultimate game against Grimsby Town, it was almost unbearable with me six foot to the right of my favourite position.

Paul Gladwell – Edinburgh

239

I never went to the enclosure standing section under the old C Stand as the Station End was the place for us young guys. I remember the bovver boys were all the rage. They used to have their skinhead haircuts, bovver boots, red braces and red socks.

One day the police had got wise to the bovver boys wearing steel cap boots, so they made them take them off at the gate and they stood for the whole match in their stocking feet – the bovver boys were not happy!

That was in the days when PC Dickie Goodchild was our mate, or at least that is what the fans used to chant.

Ron Morgan – Shrewsbury

I think it was 1970/71 season when we played Fulham at the Meadow and it was at a time when skinheads were starting to make themselves known. Towards the end of the game a couple of these morons got into the Wakeman End looking for trouble and an altercation started with a particularly ugly Fulham yob goading Town supporters.

At this point a very ordinary Town supporter in collar and tie and a cardigan, who was with his young lad, took charge of the proceedings by leaping over the wall, and having grabbed the corner flag, sorted out the yob before the police carted him off.

The reason I mention this, is that it goes to exemplify something of which we have been justifiably proud at the Meadow, in that it has always been a homely, safe, family oriented ground where everyone looks out for each other.

Pete Evans – Worthenbury

My first match at the Meadow, in fact my first ever professional football match, was on a sunny spring day back in 1971 for the visit of the mighty Aston Villa. Squeezed into the old enclosure between the Centre Stand and the old concrete and breeze block dugout, it was an exciting and happy place to be.

I cannot remember any of the goals, although I know that Town won 2-1. I do vividly remember two Villa skinheads running onto the pitch and planting a couple of claret and blue balloons in the centre circle.

I also remember my dad grumbling about the Villa hooligans spilling over the wall at the Station End and seeing police with snarling dogs trying to control them – the dogs and the hoolies!

What a great introduction to watching games at a wonderful, old fashioned football ground, one which I came to appreciate and love over the next 36 years.

Russ Teece – Bayston Hill, Shrewsbury

My first game was the last game of season 1972-73. A school friend was a big Town fan and kept going on about Shrewsbury Town's Jim Holton. I had decided to go to the game against Bournemouth to see Holton v Ted MacDougal but it was postponed for some reason. When it was finally played both players had been sold and the game ended 0-0.

One of my main memories of 1973-74 was The Hollies song, 'The Air That I Breathe', echoing round the near empty terraces in the April sunshine for the games against Blackburn Rovers and Huddersfield Town. The last game of that season was memorable for me, another 0-0 draw against local rivals Walsall. It was the featured game on ATV's Star Soccer. At some point in the game the Town scored, and instantly all hell broke loose as the Walsall fans charged into the Station End from the Riverside. The Town fans around me vanished into the enclosure and I was seemingly all alone. A Walsall fan approached and demanded my silk scarf (which was tied around my wrist as was the fashion).

Now this had cost me 35p that season, and I was not going to give it up (I'm not tough but I am tight!) so I turned down his kind offer, to which he responded by nutting me, and for some reason lost in the mists of time there he was gone. At this point I decided that discretion was the better part of valour and decamped over the wall to the enclosure with my tail between my legs, but safe in the knowledge that I had kept my prized scarf and the Town had won the game.

Imagine my horror on Sunday lunchtime when I settled down to watch Star Soccer wearing dark glasses to hide my black eye, (my mum never questioned it for some reason) accompanied by the dulcet tones of Hugh Johns and found that the goal had been disallowed and the game had ended 0-0.

Charles Marrion – St. Georges, Telford

How things have changed! I can remember standing on the Riverside at an evening game against Aston Villa as a young boy, and someone near me swore. The next thing I heard was someone saying "hey there's a kid here, cut that out." And there was no segregation of fans.

Compare that to Shrewsbury v Middlesbrough in the 1980s and I was working at this one, whoever lost were relegated out of Division Two and Town scored an early goal. From there we went to the depths of police officers being deployed into the ground in full riot gear. There are rumours that this was the first time riot police were put into a ground in the country. I can remember a colleague who I went into the Station End with got kicked unconscious, and a number of others were taken to hospital. I had never seen anything like it before and am glad I have not seen anything like it since.

Yes there have been problems since at the Meadow but hopefully we are eradicating these. More families have come to the Meadow, and will continue with the move to the new ground. Coming to football should be about enjoyment and fun and not fear.

On a lighter note I remember the FA Cup win against Everton well, myself and my colleague from Everton had left the ground two minutes from the end, with the score 1-1, to keep an eye on fans leaving the ground. We were already talking of the replay at Goodison Park. Then, there was this roar and banging on the back of the Wakeman Stand. I think we both just looked at each other in total shock and just stood there thinking, "no they haven't." The fans leaving a few minutes later soon told us they had!

- And the queues for the Chelsea game up the Wyle Cop. Where will the queues for the big games go now?

There were, of course times when I went into the Riverside to sort out a problem to be greeted by a 'Knees up Mother Brown' crowd jumping up and down and my helmet disappearing into the melee. Not funny at the time, but can bring a smile to my face now.

DC Alan Roberts – Shrewsbury

SCORE SCORER
A B C D E F G H I J K
M N O P Q R S T U V W
HAWKINS
WEM
33278
PLANT HIRE
AGRICULTURAL

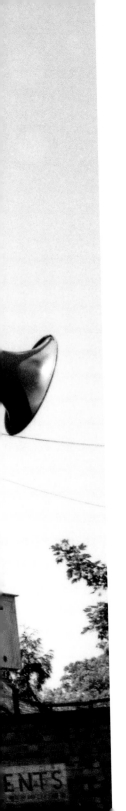

A lot has been said and written about that old blue box. No, no, not the Tardis that Doctor Who travels through time in. This blue box is the old half-time scoreboard that used to stand in the corner of the Wakeman End, and unfortunately it was not bigger on the inside than the outside like the one belonging to the Time Lord.

It was around 1980 when I first gingerly climbed the old metal ladder before reaching for the grab rail and hoisting myself onto the narrow platform, then unlatching the old wooden door to step inside. It took a few seconds for my eyes to adjust to their new darkened surroundings. I quickly realised that the Hilton it wasn't but, nevertheless, I was in awe, for I was suddenly part of the scoreboard.

I had wheedled my way in through my best mate at school, Paul Glover. His eldest brother David was the man in charge. It was very much a Glover brother project, but middle brother Steven had moved away and suddenly wasn't in attendance at every game, so Paul asked me if I would like to help.

As I looked around for the very first time, I immediately noticed the strategically placed neat rows of all the metal score plates. The other thing to strike me was the low roof. There was enough room to stand up straight provided you were not over 6'1". I was going to have to quickly learn that you could not jump up and punch the air when Town scored!

Back in those days there were no fancy communications. Our only contact with the outside world was David's old trusty portable radio. Around ten minutes before the half-time whistle, David would switch it on and scroll up and down the frequencies lightly penning in latest scores on the half-time score check in the programme, which gave the games to correspond to the letters on the scoreboard.

As the half-time scores started rolling in, David would firmly pen in the scores and shout out the letters and scores whilst we would duly put them up. It was a definite art in obtaining all the scores. There was no point waiting for Radio 2 (Radio 5 wasn't born then) to give the classified half-time scores, as invariably the second half was under way again and people lost interest in the big blue scoreboard. Back in those days it was only a ten minute interlude, so you had to be fast.

The best way was to keep changing stations picking up all the different local radio broadcasts. This of course meant you ran the risk of not picking up certain scores, and it did occasionally happen but, on the whole, the completion success rate was good.

Putting in the scores was a bit of a challenge. Some slid in with ease, others needing a little persuading to fit in the grooves, and then there were some where it was a fight to the death, hammering on them with clenched fists to 'persuade' them to go in. If people below wondered why there was all the noise up above, that was why.

If putting them in could be trying, taking them out was even worse! Cold winter fingers trying to coerce out immovable objects. Sometimes you would have to resort to the 'foot method' of dislodgement. It was all good fun.

I always had this fear of losing one of the score plates onto a head below. It thankfully never happened, but you could just imagine being sued for thousands! Another fear, in later years, was of your foot going through the ever-decaying floorboards.

There were a couple of spots where the roof leaked when it rained. Season by season, the problem gradually increased. A piece of board was put down covering the area affected, but it got to the stage you just stepped over it because there was that much give in the floorboards, they would not have withstood the full weight of a person. If only people knew, I don't think they would have sheltered underneath when the elements were being particularly unkind.

Other problems were not caused by the elements, but the changing rules of the modern game. An increase in substitutes, first of all in the FA Cup, meant the sudden need for a number 14 in case that substitute scored. The scoreboard not only showed the score but number of the goal scorer too. There was to be no brand spanking new plate provided with that on. Instead David improvised and blacked out one of the others and then carefully painted 14 in white on it.

Then Salop really threw a spanner in the works by deciding to be like a Premiership team and have squad numbers instead of 1-14 each game. That was a bridge too far as there were just not enough plates to add all the required numbers on. Improvisation was called for. If Kevin Somerfield or anyone else with a high number scored we used both the home and away scorer slots to show the two numbers required.

The end of the scoreboard was very sad indeed. There was no warning, it was just ripped up one close season and condemned to the rubbish tip. It wouldn't have happened like that nowadays. The letters on the frame, the score plates, ladder, door etc. would have been auctioned to raise a fair bit of money for the club. Unfortunately there was not that foresight at the time.

Chris Wynne – Shrewsbury

My final season at Gay Meadow has felt like something of a watershed, I have so many memories of the ground. I have been trying to make every moment count, trying to take in the atmosphere as much as possible before the final goodbye. When groundstaff asked for volunteers to help clear the snow off the pitch before the Bury match on February 11th 2007, I leapt at the chance to help try to get the game on.

Whilst it was disappointing that the game was called off, it was great to spend a few hours in the ground. I took a break and stood in the empty Riverside, taking in the atmosphere of the old place.

A great morning, taking the chance to spend a few more final hours at the Meadow.

And a great show of solidarity between the club and fans. The club and its directors showed just how much the fans meant to them, unlike some of the bigger clubs where fans are nowadays seen as paying customers.

Chris Czora – Shrewsbury

When attending a game at Telford United in the Conference season, I collapsed when leaving my seat. I suffered a dislocated left kneecap and needed a full quad repair of my left knee. After receiving morphine for the pain, I was rushed to the Princess Royal Hospital to reset my kneecap and undergo knee surgery. I remained in the PRH for quite a few days until the Tuesday night of the Chester City game at Gay Meadow.

Unfortunately, I contracted a bug whilst in the hospital and on the day of the match they would not discharge me. However, against medical advice, I got my brother from Bayston Hill to collect me at 6.30pm and drop me straight off at Gay Meadow. Straight from my hospital bed to a Gay Meadow seat, crutches and all. My less than understanding wife, coming from Wistanstow in South Shropshire, collected me at the end of the game to finally take me home.

Colin James – Wistanstow

In the late 70s and early 80s I used to stand in the old Enclosure with my dad and two sisters. It used to be absolutely packed. I remember one game when my sister fainted. She was passed over everyone's head down to the front and was carried up to the dugout to be revived. I remember feeling very jealous because she had been so near to the manager and players. I don't think I was very sympathetic.

David Morgan – Endon, Stoke-on-Trent

Fred was a chap in his mid-seventies, Shrewsbury born and bred. He used to make his own coracles and I remember him cycling down to the Meadow from his Monkmoor home, with the coracle strapped over his shoulders. He made one just for me and taught me how to paddle it during the summer of around 1985-86. This was around the time that he was winding down and didn't really fancy going down the treacherous river bank to get into the boat. Both of us have ended up in the Severn at some stage – and both as a result of getting in or out of the coracle!

We would sit alongside the dugout, and in later years the 'No-go' area, and wait for the ball to be kicked out of the ground – 50p per returned ball in those days! The coracle would already be waiting in the 'No-go' area of the ground. Once the ball had been kicked out, we'd make our way, with the coracle, through the door in the Station End and down onto the river bank, some mean feat in itself as the bank was more often than not very muddy. It was then a case of very carefully getting into the boat and paddling out to where the ball was. All we then had to do was guide the ball to the coracle using the paddle, and reach to pick it out of the Severn – not easy when you're trying to balance. It was then a case of getting back to the riverbank, throwing the ball onto the bank, and trying to get

yourself, and the boat, out of the water. Now that was harder than getting in and that would be when we would end up in the river.

A couple of funny stories that spring to mind – Fred went off down the river in the coracle after the ball one winter's night. It was cold and misty, and the river was high. He paddled and paddled and eventually caught up with the 'ball' on the weir side of the railway bridge. However when he reached out for the 'ball', it took off and flew away. He had been chasing a swan!

I also recall Shrewsbury's 10-1 win over Cefn Albion in the Welsh Cup. I'd been on a school trip that day and had gone straight to the ground in my school uniform as I hadn't had time to change. It was a rather wet night and, of course, the ball was booted over the Wakeman End. I eagerly went to fetch the ball and on the riverbank side of the corner between the Wakeman End and the Riverside were several steps. Being in my usual hurry I jumped down these steps and landed flat on my back in about 4-6 inches of mud – the river had been in flood and had only just subsided. You can only begin to imagine what reception I got when I arrived back home, caked in mud. It was bad enough walking back around the pitch in front of the supporters.

Mark Hobden – Shrewsbury

They filmed Fred running around the pitch with his coracle slung over his arm, I leaned over the wall and was struck by a glancing blow as the coracle sped past. It left me seeing stars for a minute and gave me a good lump on the head for several days, much to the amusement of my friends.

Anyway, it's probably fair to say that I am the only person ever to have been hit over the head by a coracle at a football match!

David Hawksworth – West Yorkshire

Over the years much was made in the media about our coracle and Fred Davies. However for me, it was the norm. In the second year of junior school, I rose with delight to the top of our class after our teacher asked if anyone knew what a coracle was, before we embarked on an afternoon of history.

Not only did I know what one was, I went on to tell my class they were made out of a framework of wood and covered with something like horse skin, and finished off with tar to waterproof it.

How I wished my mother had been there. She always battled with my dad in wanting me to go shopping with her. Being a Shrewsbury Town fan helped me with my education.

Karl Anderson – Wolverhampton

Growing up in Shrewsbury I thought all clubs who had a river running adjacent to the ground had a coracle man. I could never understand why there was so much interest in him. As I left Shrewsbury and began socalising with other football fans during my mid-twenties, they always mentioned Fred, at which I got embarrased.

Now I live back in Shrewsbury with my family, it is only now I realise how special Fred Davies was to Shrewsbury Town Football Club. A picture of him in his coracle holding up the ball is as iconic as the Wakeman School and is a part of Gay Meadow.

Fred symbolises Gay Meadow and we should cherish that fact.

Matthew Young – Shrewsbury

It was in the early '70s when I first started going down to the Meadow to follow the Town. For some strange reason they used to play on a Saturday afternoon for the first-half of the season, and then play on a Friday night after Christmas.

I was an eleven year old avid Town fan who as a member of the scouts had meetings on a Friday night. My dad was quite a disciplinarian and insisted I should honour my commitment to the scouts, which meant missing the games.

When scouts finished I would bike down to watch the last ten minutes when the gates opened, and then buy a bag of chips and scratchings from the chippy under the railway bridge.

Of course, the pull of seeing those floodlights beaming on my way to scouts, seeing the crowds walking to Gay Meadow, the smell of tobacco in the cold night air, plus those chips, eventually became too much.

The atmosphere of some cracking night games in the days of Alfie Wood was too much to miss. I ended up bunking scouts when the Town were at home and going to the matches in my scout uniform, with my Town scarf around my waist which I had hidden under my coat until I was out of the house.

As soon as I left scouts, Shrewsbury stopped playing on Friday nights which was just typical, but a shame at the same time.

Rob Fox – Shrewsbury

HOT DRINKS	
TEA	1.40
COFFEE	1.40
BOVRIL	1.40
HOT CHOC	1.40
SOUP	1.40
MINERAL WATER	1.70
COLD DRINKS	
COKE/DIET COKE	1.70
PURE ORANGE JUICE	1.00
LUCOZADE SPORT	1.60
RIBENA 500ml bottle	1.90
CONFECTIONERY	
CRISPS	.80
PASTILLES FAMILY PACK	1.90
YORKIE BAR	.90
KIT~KAT CHUNKY	.50
POLO CLEAR ICE MINT BAG	1.70

HOT SNACKS	
BURGER	2.60
CHEESEBURGER	2.80
HOT DOG	2.70
VARIOUS PIES	2.30
PASTIES TRADITIONAL VEGETARIAN	2.20
SAUSAGE ROLL	2.00
ADDITIONAL ITEMS AVAILABLE	
CHICKEN BALTI PIE	2.30
POWERADE	1.80
SMARTIES GIANT BAG	1.90
MUNCHIES BAG	1.90

Going down the Meadow for the final time it suddenly hit. I turned down the Narrows and felt my eyes well up. I would never do this again. Never stroll from the Telepost five minutes after kick-off with my mates, anticipating victory but seeing defeat. Never see the floodlights shine like stars in the night sky. All that campaigning, all those hopes and dreams, and this was it, no more.

Adrian Plimmer – Shrewsbury

So it's onwards and upwards, and whilst we will never forget the memories the old ground held for us, it is now time to start making new ones.

Gareth Hopkins - Welshpool

Gay Meadow - rest in peace, and thank you for the many memories, happy and sad, that you have given me.

Chris Czora - Shrewsbury

Grandads passed their feelings down
to siblings fullsome praise,
and now those folks support the Town
until their dying days.
Stands grew up when times were good
and floodlights lit the sky,
the river often came to flood
and leaves in autumn lie.
I've seen joys of proud promotions
witnessed relegation's tear,
but been proud of our emotions
as we've hung in year by year.
I've seen awful acts of diving
and seen streaker's hairy bums,
centre halves down hurt and writhing
as they catch one in the plums.
I've seen internationals calm and cool
to young lads first time nerves,
Arsenal, Chelsea, Liverpool
and Meole Brace reserves.
Of all our lads I've loved the most
I've been so much impressed -
our wondrous blue and amber ghost
King Arthur was the best.
But now my beams are rusting
my paintwork's flaking too,
my toilets smell disgusting
I just know my time is through.
I hope you've all enjoyed it here
you've been Shrewsbury Town and proud,
your support tremendous and sincere
you're one fantastic crowd.
But now a new beginning
with good fortune that you're owed,
with a team I hope that's winning
reborn in Oteley Road.
So now my time is at an end
it's time to go I guess,
to you my ever faithful friend -
goodbye, good luck, God bless.

Cuzz - Whitchurch

254

ACKNOWLEDGEMENTS

Shrewsbury Town Football Club (www.shrewsburytown.com) – Steve Wellbeloved, Alan Stephenson, Ian Whitfield, Joan Fox, Clive Parry. The Shrewsbury Town internet community for providing the stories and memories. Blue and Amber Messageboard (www.blue-and-amber.co.uk and http://blueandamber.proboards48.com), ShrewsChat (www.shrewschat.com). Jim Lockwood (www.lockwoodandson.co.uk) Christian Aernout, Catherine Ivill, Mike Jones, Steve Green, Mark Hobden, Chris Smith, Ron Morgan, Bob Edwards, Paul Knapton, Michael Regan, Andrew Cowie, Robin Parker, Andrew Todd. Peter Robinson and Monte Fresco MBE who were the inspiration behind this project.
POETRY Cuzz of Whitchurch. **PROOF READERS** Catherine Ivill, Tracy Piper-Wright, Steve Rogerson, Jayne Bebb, Ian Wright, Peter Taylor, Mike Ashton, Terry Jones, Chris Czora, Murray James, Paul Williams, Ron Morgan, Barbara Ashton, Dom Kirby.

PICTURE CREDITS

Action Images (www.actionimages.com) p201. **Catherine Ivill** (www.amasportsphotoagency.com) p244a, p244b, p244c. **Colorsport** (www.colorsport.co.uk) p42, p81a, p128a-b. **Fotosports International** (www.fotosports.com) Roger Parker p201, p246. **Matthew Ashton** Front cover, back cover b, p3b, p4-5, p6, p7a-b, p8, p9a, p9b, p10a-b-c, p11, p12, p13, p14, p15, p16a-b, p17a-b, p18, p19b, p20, p21, p22, p23, p24-25, p26a-b, p27, p28, p29a-b-c, p30a-b, p31, p32, p33a-b, p34, p35, p36a-b, p37, p38, p40, p41a-b, p43, p44a-b, p45, p47, p48, p50a-b-c, p51, p52, p53, p54a-b, p55, p56, p57, p58a-b, p59, p60, p61a-b-c, p62a-b, p63, p64, p65, p66a-b, p67a-b, p68, p69, p70a-b, p71a-b, p72-73, p74, p75, p76, p77, p78a-b, p79, p80a-b, p81b, p82, p83a-b, p84, p85, p86, p87, p88b-c, p89a-b-c, p89d, p90a-b, p91, p92, p93a-b, p94, p95a-b, p96, p97a-b-c, p98-99. p100-101, p103, p104, p105a-b, p106, p108, p110-111, p112, p113, p114, p115a-b, p116, p117, p118, p119, p120, p121, p122, p124, p125a-b, p127, p129a-b-c, p130a-b, p131, p132b, p133a-b-c, p134, p135, p136, p137a, p138a-b, p139, p140, p141, p142a-b, p144, p145, p146, p147, p148, p150, p151, p152a-b, p155, p156, p157, p158, p160, p161, p162, p163, p164a-b, p165a-b-c, p166a-b, p168a-b, p169, p171, p172, p173, p175a-b-c, p176a-b-c, p177a-b-c, p178, p179, p180, p181a-b, p182a-b-c, p183, p185, p186, p187, p189, p190a-b-c, p191a-b, p192, p193a-b, p194-195, p196a-b, p197a-b, p198, p199, p202a-b, p203, p204a-b, p205, p208, p210, p211, p212, p213a, p214b, p215, p216a-b-c, p217, p218, p219b, p220b, p221, p222, p223a-b-c-d, p224, p225, p226a-b, p228, p229a-b-c, p230, p231a-b, p232a-b, p233, p234, p235, p237, p238-239, p240, p241, p242, p245, p247a-b, p248a, p249, p250, p251, p252a-b-c, p253, p255, p256. **Paul Knapton** p39. **Shropshire Newspapers Ltd** (www.shropshirestar.co.uk) p126a-b, p167a-b, p219a, p227a-b. **Unknown Photographer** (All pictures sourced from Shrewsbury Town FC or picture donations to Matthew Ashton – every effort has been made to establish the rightful copyright holder) Back cover a, p3a, p19a, p46, p88a, p109, p123a-b, p132a, p137b, p143a-b, p149, p153, p154, p159, p188, p206a-b, p207a-b, p209, p220a, p248b.

References to Simon Inglis – The Football Grounds of Britain published by HarperCollins Publishers Ltd in 1996 ISBN 978-0002184267
All reasonable attempt has been made to ensure this information is correct. If there are any errors please contact the publisher at the address on page 2
The views expressed in this book are the views of the contributing fans and do not necessarily reflect the views or policies of the publisher or Shrewsbury Town FC

SUBSCRIBERS: GRAHAM PEARSE BRYAN SHERWOOD K P WYATT DAVID RUSCOE COLIN STOREY GARY HOWORTH DANA POWER BARRY DAVIES PAUL FRANCE DAVID MIDDLETON DENNIS SCARISBRICK MICHAEL TENCH MARTIN BERRY MICHAEL CANIL PAM KEVEREN ANDREW MILLER MARK BROOKER JAMES BELLAMY STEVEN PARRY JOHN & SARAH GROVE G N L MASSEY IAN HARTSHORN DR D S PINCHES ADRIAN JENNINGS PAUL ROBERTS NICOLAS O'LEARY GRAHAM SCOTT ALAN BURGE GARY EDWARDS CLAIRE GROVES D GILMOUR DAVID COLE MICHELLE BOWDLER MATTHEW CRUMP LEE BLOWER VINCE JONES BOB EDWARDS MICHAEL BROWN GAVIN TAYLOR PAUL HUBBARD ROGER GROVES LINDA BROMILOW DAVE BEIGHTON GRAHAM SMITHSON DAVID PICKEN GARETH JONES MR C RALPHS C W MARRION TOM WEBSTER KEVIN BRIGHT TERENCE FELTUS ROY THOMBS CHRISTOPHER CARPENTER D A MITCHELL ROBERT GRIFFITHS DR J GRAY STEPHEN JOHNSON ANDREW WOODYATT JOHN INGRAM MR A FLAHERTY SHIRLEY ELLIOTT JOHN PEARL MICK HUFFA JILL LUCAS PAUL J DAVIES MR R GILMORE HELEN HALL JULIAN WESTWOOD DAVID HAWKSWORTH BILL EMBREY PAUL JONES MR P BOWEN MR T J BAMFORD MR G JAMES SIMON PARRY PETER C BUTTERS JOHN LANE WILLIAM GRECH PATRICK TOMLINSON HARRY J WILSON JOHN NASH ROGER & SAM RIDGWAY E J MARTIN JOSEPH OLLERTON B DAVIES SARAH MORGAN MR I MILLER BARRY HAWKINS ROY HOPE JOHN E MATTHIAS MR R F WALKER MR D TRANTER MR R GRETTON RICHARD CROWLEY DAVID GROUCOTT MR M P SCHORAH GRAHAM FURBER MARK CHARLTON DEBBIE MORRIS JAMES REEKIE IAN BLOCKSIDGE REV A G A DORRICOTT MBE LEE W GRIFFITHS STEPHEN THOMAS BOWEN CRAIG KYNASTON PHILIP KYNASTON STEPHEN PRICE ANDREW GROVES MR C V PERKINS M J FONE GWYN EVANS PAM COE RICHARD STOCKEN MR R J DAVIES L G E DICKINS MR P J PURSLOW MR P A OVENS CARL OWEN PHILIP DAVIES JOHN MCINTYRE PHILLIP BRISBOURNE KENNETH JOHN DAVIES DAVID ASHLIN ROBERT SANDILANDS LES PHILLIPS CAROLINE WALKER CLIVE MORGAN GEOFF DAVIES STEVEN GALLIER DR P MORGAN MR J A PITCHFORD DUNCAN JONES C BRADLEY GRAHAM HUGHES PAULINE & DYLAN HUGHES LAURA POUNTNEY KEITH FRASER PAUL HASTINGS DAVE ARMITAGE MR G MCKENZIE STEVEN OLIVER DENNIS SMITH MR J WOOLLEY ALAN CARTER STEPHEN CARTER JOHN HAMILTON SUE ARCHER HOWARD ARCHER IAN ROBINSON PAUL KNAPTON RICHARD COOPER D ROSS A J BAKER SAM TAYLOR DEREK TINKLER IAN TAYLOR LEE PARTON STUART RICHARDS ALAN HUGHES DAVID CAMPION DAPHNE JONES JASON GITTINS CHRISTOPHER LLOYD GRAHAM DAVID BRIAN DUDLEY TIM HANAN D C STOCKTON DAVID ROWSON PAUL HIGGINSON PAUL JEFFRIES PATRICK LEAHY HOWARD THORNE IAN JONES A BUTLER KEITH ELCOCK PHILIP JONES SHEILA DOWNES MR SKIPWORTH JANET MOORE SHEILA SCHNELLMANN BARRY MACKLIN PAT SHAKESPEARE STEPHEN WHITTALL ALAN MANFORD DANIEL MARK RIDGWAY J K HOBLEY NICOLA ARMSTRONG ANDREW PEARCE ROB SHERWOOD-SMITH BRIAN BURNS MARK ALMOND MARK MARTIN ROGER FARRINGTON SIMON ARTHUR DOMINIC PEATON-EVANS JULIANA BERGEL MR S BENYON PETER NEALE NICHOLAS MARTIN LYN HOUGH MARTIN MILLS P BUCKLEY RICHARD COLE ROBERT THOMPSON CATHERINE EDWARDS C T HOWELL DAVID LEWIS GARETH JONES R FORMSTONE DAVID KNIGHT PETER WALDEN STEVEN DAVISON M TURNER COLIN SMITH DAVID C SMITH MISS H DUNN IAN BARBER ANTHONY BEAL DENNIS ATHERSMITH NIGEL PRICE ROBBIE BURNETT MR R N MORGAN MR M BAYLEY JONATHAN CARNEY PETER FRANCIS MR P E L JONES JOHN EDWARDS MARK HOBDEN MR M PAMMENT AMY RILEY RICHARD HOBBS MR P W BELL JAMES L WHITTALL PETER CHADWICK BRIAN MAGEE TONY JONES ANDREW MASSEY NORMAN SKEDGE TONY TYRER BRYN HOLLOWAY NIGEL ROWLAND MR M BALL DALE SKITT COLIN JACKSON THOMAS STANHOPE GODFREY JONES GEORGE OWEN JONATHAN TAYLOR DOMINIC KIRBY NAYLAND SOUTHORN IAN & PAUL MAY MR C A HAYES TRISH WRIGHT M J FONE MR J R DAY MR GLADWELL MRS J WILSON RUTH WILLIAMS JONATHAN SUTTON DEREK EVANS PETER PRICE A J JENKINSON NICHOLAS MARTIN P LANGTON COLIN BLOOMFIELD MRS S J RHODES SHARON WILLIAMS J SAYCE JOHN BERRY W P MORRIS MR R W GROVES GRAHAM HUGHES MRS W WILLIAMS ROBERT FURNISS DAVID EDWARDS MRS B MAXTON ANDREW MUIR A J PULFORD DAVID FLETCHER ALAN COLLINS P B DAVIES MIKE HALL MICHELLE RUSHTON CHRIS EDWARDS IAN ROGER JONES RICHARD POWELL MARK THORNTON MR REECE MR G WINTER CHRIS FLETCHER PAT ALLBUARY G N HARRIS PETER WALDEN KEITH HONEYFIELD RICHARD PRICE PHILIP & MATHEW MEAD R J PARSONS MICHAEL QUINN COLIN W JONES DARREN HILTON A TAYLOR GARY BRIGHT ROBERT MANLEY STUART ROBERTS DAWN CANK MRS V BLAND DEREK GRIFFITHS STEVE PRICE GEORGE TAYLOR DAVID HARTLEY DAVE WEBSTER GILL TURNER NEIL CHIDLOW KEVIN JONES MR DAVIES STEPHEN HUTCHISON B J OWEN J M WILLIAMS DAVE WHITTALL MATTHEW HARRIS MARK JONES RON MORGAN ROBERT FOX COLIN SAYCE PHIL VENABLES KIERON SEABRONE SONIA BUTTERLEY JIM DAVIES IAN MEREDITH MRS DIXON MR & MRS A FERRIDAY MR D J WINTER NORMAN BISSELL GRAHAM STFC DAVID SMITH FREDDIE EVANS TONY PRITCHARD BRYAN ALLEN HELEN & DARRELL CORFIELD MAURICE TAYLOR ERIC TAYLOR M P BOND MR GRANDA BARRY DAVIES MIKE EVANS MR GOLIGHTLY ERIC DAVIES STUART HUNTING NEILL PASCO DAVID EDWARDS DENISE FIELDING DAVID MATTHIAS GEFFREY SCOTT LORD PHILLIP DAVIES E.J HEATH STUART EVERAY JULIE BANCE KEVIN DAVIES PHIL LANGSTAFF MARK MCINTYRE MR P MCGOWAN JOHN RAWNSLEY STEPHEN BENNETT ELIZABETH SMALL KEITH BURGE MR R.J SPREY J HAMMONDS MR PHILIP HUGHES MR ROY BAUGH STUART CROCKER BOB BURFORD STEVE PARRY MRS OWEN ALAN TURNER TIM WORLEY DR A M CROFT ANTHONY MULLINEUX GRAHAM DALY JOHN HOWARTH